THE COMPLEAT STRAWBERRY

THE STRAWBERRY PLANT

The rootless strawberry plant
Moves across the soil. It hops
Six inches. Has no single location,
Or root.
You cannot point to its origin,
Or parent. It shoots out
A pipe, and one more plant
Consolidates its ground.
It puts out crude petals, loosely met,
As if the business of flowering
Were to be got over. Their period is brief.
Even then, the fruit is green,
Swart, hairy. Its petals invite tearing
And are gone quickly.
As if they had been. The fruit swells,
Reddens, becomes succulent.
Propagation through the devouring
Appetite of another.
Is sweet, seeded, untruculent;
Slugs like it, all over.
It is nubile to the lips,
And survives even them. And teeth,
Insane with edible fury,
Of the loving kind.

Jon Silkin, 'Nature With Man', 1965

Opposite: Border by Jean Bourdichon, French, born 1547.

Overleaf: 'Prolific Hautbois', Anon

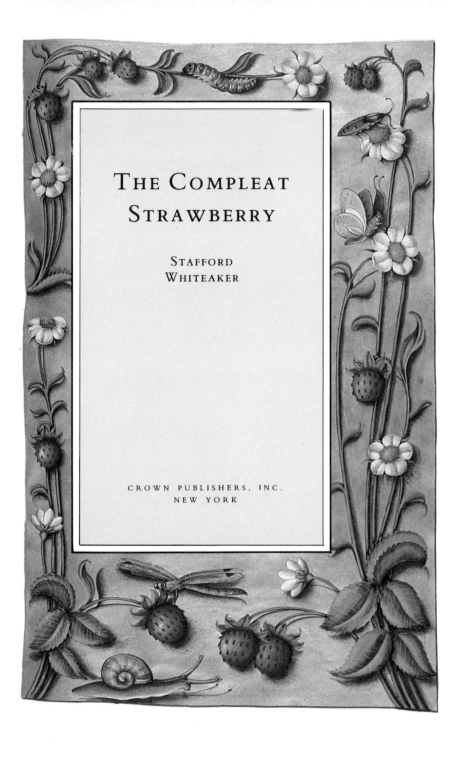

THE COMPLEAT
STRAWBERRY

STAFFORD
WHITEAKER

CROWN PUBLISHERS, INC.
NEW YORK

FOR MY SON, ALEXANDER

Designed by Philippa Bramson
Picture Research by Jenny de Gex

Published in the United States in 1985 by Crown Publishers, Inc., One Park Avenue, New York, New York 10016 and simultaneously in Canada by General Publishing Company Limited

Originally published in Great Britain under the title THE COMPLEAT STRAWBERRY by Century Publishing Co. Ltd., Portland House, 12 – 13 Greek Street, London W1V 5LE
CROWN is a trademark of Crown Publishers, Inc.

Library of Congress Cataloging in Publication Data

Whiteaker, Stafford.
The compleat strawberry.

Includes index.
1. Strawberries. 2. Cookery (Strawberries) 3. Strawberries — Folklore.
4. Strawberries — Therapeutic use. 5. Strawberries in art. I. Title.,
SB385.W59 1985   634'.75   85-5939
ISBN 0-517-55926-9

10 9 8 7 6 5 4 3 2 1

First American Edition
Manufactured in Great Britain

Contents

'The Woodman's Daughter' by Sir John Everett Millais (1826–1896)

ONE

THE STORY OF THE STRAWBERRY

> The Strawberrie with his small and slender
> hearie branches, creepeth alongst the ground.
> *Rembert Dodoens (1516–1585)*

Over two hundred years ago people first began developing new varieties of strawberry, but the wild one is still supreme in both taste and smell.

From the mountains of Asia to the woods of England, the strawberry in its many varieties ripens above the low orchard of its own leaves, heralding its presence with a fragrance that has inspired the poets. Keats dreamt of an idyllic state where he would 'sleep in the grass, feed upon apples red and strawberries and choose each pleasure that my fancy sees'. Bacon felt that the scent of dying strawberry leaves was second only to those of the violet and musk rose, and suggested a connection between such sweet smells and the very sound of music.

Grown only to be devoured, the strawberry is more than a food: it is the fruit of saints, a symbol of nobility, and the stuff of myths. With its perfumed fruit, red and ripe in the warm airs of summer, just waiting to be eaten, it is little wonder that the strawberry should be the symbol of Venus, goddess of love.

THE WILD STRAWBERRY

The strawberry belongs to the genus *Fragaria*, a member of the rose family, Rosaceae, which includes roses, apples and plums.

The name *Fragaria* comes from the Latin *fragga*, which is derived from *fragars*, 'fragrant'. The genus is so widely distributed that its fruits are gathered by the Laplanders in the Arctic and by the people of India. Cultivated strawberries as we know them have a comparatively short history, but Ovid noted both the wood and alpine strawberries and Pliny mentioned the plant as one of the few native fruits of Italy. Jean-Anthelme Brillat-Savarin remarked in *La Physiologie du Goût* (1825) that '. . . a great ambition among wealthy Romans was to have beautiful gardens in which they cultivated not only the fruits known but also . . . the strawberry from the valleys of Mount Ida'. This berry of Asia Minor is exquisite. Even today, when ships put in to port in Corfu (Kerkyra), if you are lucky and the captain lingers a few hours, local people may come aboard bearing a leaf or a piece of paper cupped in their hands filled with these tiny wild strawberries. When you hold the fruit up to your nose, the fragrance is overpowering.

The origin of the English name 'strawberry' is something of a mystery. There is no corresponding word in any other Teutonic language – most have a variation on 'earth-berry'. The present word is derived from the Anglo-Saxon *stréawberige*. The belief that the name is a reference to the practice of laying straw under the plants to protect the berries from soil and pests has no factual basis. The name may refer to the plant's straying runners, since '*stréaw*' can be taken to mean 'strew' rather than 'straw'. Webster's Dictionary, on the other hand, along with many others, takes a more literal approach, claiming that the name refers to the tiny straw-like seeds (achenes) found on the fruit.

The part of the strawberry which we think of as the fruit is in fact a false fruit, a receptacle at the end of the flower stalk. The tiny achenes on its surface are the true fruits of the plant. Sir John Hill, in his *The British Herbal: A History of Plants and Trees, Natives of Britain, Cultivated for Use, or Raised for Beauty* (1756), writes that 'in the strawberry the seeds are displayed quite otherwise. They are neither surrounded by juice nor covered with a skin, they sit naked on the outside of the fruit.'

While we know that the wild strawberry grew in prehistoric times, because fossilized achenes have been found, it was not widely cultivated in ordinary gardens until comparatively recently except in Peru, where the plant was brought early on from the wild into deliberate cultivation. Our ancestors gathered the wild or wood strawberry, *Fragaria vesca*, whose

*'Choix des Plus Belles Fleurs' by P. J.
Redouté, Paris 1827. Right:
'Hautbois' by Jacques Le Moyne de
Morgues, c. 16th century*

several varieties are to be found all over northern Europe. It is a tall, erect
plant, with long, slender and rather numerous runners; its leaves are silky
at first but rough in maturity. The flowers are small and borne irregularly;
the fruit is small, either red or white, and of outstanding flavour. William
Salmon, in his *Botanologia: The English Herbal, or History of Plants* (1710),
wrote: 'The First or Wood Strawberry are very red when they are ripe,
and of a pleasant Winy taste. The Berries of the Wood Kind are very red,
and the smallest of all the sorts.'

The passion of the French for *fraises de bois* (wood strawberries) has
lasted for centuries. The *fraises de bois*, which are still to be found growing
in the wild, are always to be preferred to berries from the garden: despite
all the horticultural development of the strawberry, the flavour of the wild
fruit has yet to be improved upon. In North America, the berry in its true
form is found only in the eastern United States as an escape from gardens.
There is, however, a race of wild strawberry, *Fragaria vesca americana*,
which is native in the New World from Newfoundland down to the
Carolinas and to the west as far as the Great Plains.

THE STRAWBERRY IN MYTH AND LORE

Any plant used over the centuries for medicinal purposes gains a certain mythological reputation and the wild strawberry is no exception.

To dream of strawberries is supposed to be a good omen: if a young man does so his wife will be sweet-tempered and bear him many children, all boys.

In Teutonic legend the strawberry was sacred to the goddess Frigga, principal wife of Odin. As goddess of the clouds in the sky and of married love, she ruled all housewives and is often depicted with housekeeper's keys dangling from her girdle. It was said that she stole children who had died, concealed them in strawberries and sent them thus packaged on clouds up to heaven.

Many fairy tales involve the gathering of strawberries, often out of season, when danger lurks in the winter snows. One of the best known is 'Three Little Men in the Woods' by the Brothers Grimm. A cruel stepmother sends her stepdaughter out in a paper dress on a bitter day, ordering her to go into the woods and pick strawberries – and not to come back without some. The child wanders through the snow until finally she finds a house in the middle of the forest. Three little men tell her to come inside to get warm. She shares a meagre meal with them and is then given a broom to sweep the snow from the door. Under the snow she finds beautiful red berries. She picks the magic berries and runs home.

A German fable tells of a child going into the woods to pick strawberries for her sick mother. The girl meets a beautiful lady magnificently dressed in golden moss who asks her for some of the scant collection of fruit. The child kindly gives some to her, and as a reward the berries are returned to her in the form of gold.

In Bavaria peasants apparently believe that elves are fond of strawberries: they tie little baskets filled with wild berries to the horns of their cattle, in this way hoping to please the elves so that they will make the livestock prosper.

Man has always created myths surrounding birthmarks. Modern medicine calls the strawberry birthmark a vascular naevus which is visible at or soon after birth, but once upon a time it was thought to be the mark of royalty. Both Homer and the Emperor Augustus had one, and Pliny decided that it was a hereditary transmission.

Mary holding out a strawberry to the Infant Jesus, Hours of Tours (Paris, 1514)

Some folk traditions credited the Moon with originating such birthmarks. In Persian culture they were considered 'notes of beauty', and one of Cervantes' heroines sports a strawberry mark which Don Quixote finds enticing.

In the Christian tradition the strawberry became a symbol of both the Virgin Mary and John the Baptist, who was said to have lived for a time on strawberries. This latter tale could possibly be true, as various strands of the legend overlap. For example on St John's Day mothers of children who have died in infancy are supposed to take care not to eat strawberries for fear that the Virgin Mary, thus deprived of her favoured fruit, will refuse the children entry into heaven. There is an echo here of the legend about Frigga.

Since the strawberry was the fruit of the Virgin Mary, and was associated in myths and folklore with goodness and purity, it came to symbolize these attributes in the signs of European rank and aristocracy. In Britain it was incorporated into the designs for the coronets of the nobility: eight strawberry leaves for a duke or an earl and four for a marquis. High honour indeed for the modest strawberry.

In the coat of arms of Simon, Lord Fraser of Lovat, as it appeared in the reign of the Holy Roman Emperor Charles II, the Bald (823–877), five strawberry flowers are arranged in the form of a St Andrew's Cross. Above his shield appear 'strawberry leves a lacing argent'. It is said that these arms were created because a noble ancestor pleased the French king with a dish of wild strawberries. The Lovats' motto, *Je suis prest* ('I am ready'), applies perfectly to a ripe strawberry.

AN EXPENSIVE FOOD

The strawberries sold in the streets were usually done up in little pottles, which were straw baskets shaped like a cone; they held about half a pint. The pottles were carried strung on long poles. As far back as 1530 we find recorded in the Privy Purse Expenses of Henry VIII the purchase of 'a pottle of strawberries for 10d'.

Before the age of mechanized transport, strawberries were brought to London for sale by women carrying baskets of the fruit on their heads. Many of these women were from Shropshire and so they became known, in general, wherever their origin, as 'Shropshire girls'. They travelled in groups of perhaps twenty or thirty and were noted for their speed, moving along at what we today call jogging pace.

While there must have been a margin of safety in buying strawberries gathered from the wild, there was no knowing how dirty the fingers that had picked them or handled them might have been.

Hygiene apart, fruit was not and had not been highly regarded as a food in England. Indeed, in his 1698 *Mémoires et observations faites par un voyageur en Angleterre . . .* , Francis Misson de Valbourg remarks on the fact that in England fruit was rarely seen as a dessert: '. . . the dessert they never dream of, unless it be a piece of cheese. Fruit is brought only to the Tables of the Great, and of the small Number even among them.' J. C. Drummond, in *The Englishman's Food* (1939), commented that when fruit was eaten 'it was usually with the idea that it was useful to "keep down the vapours"'.

Part of the reason for this was expense – although, as long ago as the fifteenth century, trade with the East had brought down the price of sugar

Victorian artists like James Catnach and others, were able to ignore poverty and idealized the London criers as they sang out their strawberries:

Rare ripe strawberries and
Hautboys, sixpence a pottle.
Full to the bottom, hautboys.
Strawberries and Cream are
charming and sweet
Mix them and try how delightful
they eat.

*Charles Hindley 'Life and Times
of James Catnach' 1878*

and thereby helped popularize the serving of fruit tarts and puddings after meat courses. None the less, while people often seem to assume that during the sixteenth, seventeenth, and eighteenth centuries only imported fruits like oranges and lemons were expensive, native fruits could be too. Gooseberries, for example, cost the household of the Earl of Bedford 6d. for four pints in 1663 – a prohibitive price for an ordinary working man who might earn a shilling a day.

The accounts for the wedding dinner of John Verney* – for seven people at the Rummer in London's Queen Street in 1680 – illustrate the cost of strawberries in comparison with other foods, including imported ones.

	£	s	d		£	s	d
Beer – ayle	0	3	0	2 Rabets	0	3	0
Wine	0	11	0	A dish of peese	0	6	0
Orings	0	1	0	8 hartey Chokes	0	5	0
A dish of fish	1	0	0	A dish of Strabreys	0	6	0
2 Geese	0	8	6	A dish of Chereys	0	5	6
4 fatt Chikens	0	8	0				

In *The Fruit and Vegetable Markets of the Metropolis* (1896) W. W. Glenny makes special mention of the London strawberry markets: 'Among the past curiosities of the London markets was the system whereby the metropolis was supplied with strawberries. The supply was chiefly from the neighbourhoods of Isleworth, Brentford, Ealing, Hammersmith, Fulham and Mortlake, where were nearly a thousand acres of garden ground appropriated to the growing of this fruit for the metropolis. From about the middle of May in each year, the strawberry-trade afforded employment to a large number of women, who assembled in the gardens as soon as daylight appeared, and commenced plucking the fruit; the best fruit was taken to the packing room, and carefully put into pottles; fifty or sixty of these were placed in a larger basket; and before seven o'clock in the morning the women were despatched to the metropolis, each bearing a large basket supported by a cushion on her head. The weight of these laden baskets varied from 30 lb. to 40 lb.; and yet those sturdy dames trotted along at an astounding pace – not walking, not running, but at something between the two, which enabled them to cover five miles within the hour'.

* Rendered in Margaret M. Verney's *Memoirs of the Verney Family*, Vol. IV, 1899.

Victorian strawberry pickers in fields near Sittingbourne

The quantity of strawberries consumed by Londoners grew every year. In 1849 Mayhew, in his *Morning Chronicle*, told of '600,000 pottles of strawberries' being sold between the Covent Garden, Spitalfields and Farringdon markets, and a year later Braithwaite Poole recorded that seven hundred tons of strawberries were being sold annually through the London marketplaces – especially the 'fruit-laden arcade of Covent Garden'. In 1873 a single London firm used two hundred tons of strawberries in its production of jams and preserves.

EARLY STRAWBERRY CULTIVATION

Out of more than a hundred varieties of the strawberry plant, only *Fragaria vesca* and three others – *F. viridis, F. chiloensis* and *F. elatior* – became cultivated. These are the main characters in the story of the creation of the modern strawberry.

FRAGARIA VESCA

The Saxon medical work, the *Leechbook of Bald*, written in the tenth century, mentions the strawberry; and the fruit appears again in two different manuscripts related to Edward III in the period 1328–1329. In comparison with other wild food-plants native to Europe which were cultivated in the garden, the strawberry is a newcomer, probably not introduced until the end of the thirteenth century. Early records of the strawberry's cultivation are rare but we do know that by about this time it was being seriously grown. A record of 1324 from a northern French hospital notes tne planting of strawberries and one of the first illustrations of the cultivated strawberry appeared as early as 1454 in the Mainz *Herbarius*.

The growing of vegetables and fruit in the gardens of big houses became fashionable towards the end of the sixteenth century. The wild strawberry was well established in these gardens and in London the fruit was available both from market gardens and from the wild. Considering the poor keeping quality of the strawberry and the difficulties of transporting it in those days, it is hardly surprising that the rich wanted direct access to the plants. Yet, for all this cultivation, Thomas Hyll, as late as the 1560s, noted in *The Profitable Arte of Gardening* that 'the strawberrie is counted among those herbs that grow in the fieldes of their owne accorde'.

And Edward Hyams, a modern authority on the strawberry, points out that Olivier de Serres, in *Théatre d'Agriculture* (1600), recommended the gardener to seek fresh strawberry plants from the woods and to transplant these into his own garden. It was hoped that in this way the size of the fruit would be increased – but all such efforts were in vain. As Hyams remarks, although the strawberry was cultivated from around 1400 onwards, 'two centuries of gardening care had made no great improvement in this fruit'. Even in the nineteenth century the American philosopher Ralph Waldo Emerson (1803–1882) was to note in his essay 'On Prudence' that 'strawberries bluntly lose their flavor in garden beds'.

While the English brought the strawberry into their gardens very late and the French only a little earlier, there is some disagreement among historians as to when the plant was brought into cultivation in the ancient world around the Mediterranean basin. It seems likely that the rich of those days would have tried, like their mediaeval counterparts, to increase the plants' yield. Certainly Persian and Egyptian gardening inspired the Greeks and then, in turn, the Romans.

However, the native English strawberry was left in the woods by the majority of the population; this made good sense, for the plant grew profusely in the wild at a time when space for cultivating food was for most people restricted. Moreover, what people choose to eat – except in times of starvation – is dictated more by custom than by either taste or availability. Even by the fourteenth and fifteenth centuries the kitchen gardens of the English supplied mainly herbs, onions and leeks, and only a very limited range of fruit. Fruit was often more valued as a basis for drinks, spiced desserts, preserves and comfits, and as a laxative, rather than as a food in its own right.

Although seventy-eight plants suitable for cultivation were listed in a didactic poem by one 'Mayster Jon Gardener' in 1440, most of them were savoury herbs for the kitchen and for the making of medications. Yet there is one soft fruit mentioned in this poem, the first completely original English work on horticulture, and this fruit is, of course, the strawberry. None the less, with crude hand tools, little or no forms of mechanization, limited allocation of land for personal cultivation and the need to devote most waking hours to the creation of food, it is not surprising that the common people left the strawberries to grow wild and asked for nothing more than to be allowed to gather them in season. In addition, the strawberry does not keep or travel well; as William Cobbett noted, the strawberry is exceeded by few fruits in all aspects but one, this single aspect being its keeping ability.

During the fifteenth century the quality and amount of food available to the ordinary country person in England increased steadily, but by the latter half of the sixteenth century both had severely declined. However, the rich continued to have well laden tables. Cardinal Wolsey in 1509 rounded off a feast of porpoise with dishes of strawberries and fresh cream. In Elizabethan times, fruits including strawberries were served at special dinners. In a banquet given by the Skinners' Company in 1560 and recorded in the *Diary of Henry Machyn* (1550–1563), among the sweets noted were: 'spyse-bred, comfets sukette [fruits preserved with sugar], "marmalade" [a rare luxury, since oranges were very expensive] and "cheres" and "straberes"'.

If purchased strawberries were for the rich man's table only, gathered strawberries were for the people. Thomas Hyll, in 1593, noted that strawberries were 'much eaten at all men's tables in the summer with wine and sugar'. Still, it would be wrong to assume that everyone was gorging themselves on strawberries willy-nilly throughout the season. Scientific ignorance and folk medicine set certain limits on any such wanton indulgence. The belief that fruit and vegetables were bad for both children and adults was widespread. It was thought that the summer diarrhoea from which children of those times suffered annually was a direct result of their eating too much fruit. (In reality the upsets were a product of poor hygiene.) Orthodox medical opinion of the day advised adults, too, to be very careful about how much fruit they ate. Such admonishments were reinforced by traditional herbal medicine: if something was believed to be valuable medically, as was the strawberry plant, then it was a mistake to eat too much of it as ordinary food. However, people managed then, as now, to hold more than one view of the same thing at the same time – so everyone happily continued to imbue strawberries with powerful curative properties while delightedly eating them as food.

Not until the eighteenth century did it begin to be claimed that the eating of fruit as food, rather than just in small quantities as medicine, could be beneficial. In 1776 William Smith, a leading dietary authority, said in his *A Sure Guide in Sickness and Health* that fruit was 'the lightest most wholesome food we can eat'. Dr Cadogan, a concerned and visionary physician, in his *Essay on Nursing and Management of Children* (1750), dismissed the old belief that eating fruit was bad for children: 'I am sure all these things are wholesome and good for them.'

But only very slowly did people accept that fruit, including the strawberry, was beneficial to health. As late as 1916, 11,000 men were invalided out of the First World War suffering from scurvy.

FRAGARIA ELATIOR

From the late sixteenth century onwards English agricultural methods started to change as the Dutch, with their passion for plants, began to influence English garden design and plant cultivation. As a result, the character of English menus over the next two centuries altered considerably. In typical dinners of the 1540s vegetables were uncommon and fruit seldom served, but a hundred years later oranges, lemons and wild berries

were included as a matter of routine. Fruit was becoming popular, although vegetables lagged behind. After a further hundred years, by the middle of the 1700s, many forms of fruit and vegetables had joined the strawberry on the banqueting tables. This change is reflected in such works as John Evelyn's *Acetaria* (1699) and Hannah Glasse's *Art of Cookery Made Plain and Easy* (1747), whose excellent fruit and vegetable dishes still find favour today. After this time, as the plants and influences of the New World became part of everyday European life and as the 'scientific

'Fragaria vesca'

method' found increasing support,
the English regarded more and more
leaves, vegetables and fruit as food.

As delicious as the tiny-fruited
Fragaria vesca is, it is of no importance in the genetic history of
the modern garden strawberry
which we cultivate and buy today.
What *Fragaria vesca* did was to bring
the strawberry in from the woods
to the garden – in this way it led
towards our cultivation of quite
different strawberry species. Today *Fragaria vesca* is enjoying a revival in the form
of the alpine varieties which are being
enthusiastically grown for their superior flavour.

Other varieties of wild strawberry exist. As
happens with all plants – whether under cultivation
or growing in the wild – mutants have appeared
from time to time. For example, there was a
strawberry variant which appeared at the very end

'Sweet Cone', Anon

of the seventeenth century, *Fragaria feflagellis*, and later on there were
several other types distinguished by their possession of some peculiar
feature, such as the single-leaved *Fragaria monophylla*.

Much more important was the European wild strawberry, *Fragaria
elatior*, known when under cultivation as the *Hautbois* or 'hautboy'. The
English name seems to be a corruption of the German *Haarbeer*, the berry
being plentiful in the wild in Germany. Opinions vary but this is the
derivation of the word which I prefer.

The hautboy was introduced to England from the Continent very early
on. In *Pinax* (1623) Gaspard Bauhin mentions the 'Haarbeer of Oesner'.
From time to time the name changed: Parkinson in 1640 called it the
'Bohemian', and Stephen Switzer in his *The Practical Fruit Gardener* (1724)
called it the 'Polonian'.

Whatever they were called, hautboys were difficult to raise in the
garden, thanks to fertilization problems. In a paper read to the Royal
Horticultural Society on 4th November, 1806, Thomas Andrew Knight

(1759–1838) said, 'If nature, in any instance, permits the existence of vegetable mules – but this I am not inclined to believe – these plants seem to be beings of that kind.'

The hautboy may today be classified synonymously as *Fragaria moschata* Duchesne or *Fragaria magna* Thuill. Cultivated varieties in English gardens were named 'Globe', 'Prolific' and 'Black'; in France they were known as 'Royale', 'Framboise' and 'Abricot'. All of these berries have a distinctive musky flavour and are the type the characters in Jane Austen's *Emma* (1816) chose as the very best in Mr Knightley's garden at Donwell. In a letter from Godmersham dated Monday, 20th June, 1808, Jane told her sister Cassandra, 'I want to hear of your gathering Strawberries, we have had them three times here.'

The hautboy was once the most popular strawberry sold in England, and the street sellers used to be heard crying out, 'Hotboys! Hotboys!' Today it is still possible to find the berries, escaped long ago from the garden. The writer Edward Hyams found nearly an acre of them in Hampshire. He recalled that 'the plants grew in association with vervain and the whole valley, on a day of great heat, was full of the fragrance of strawberries.'

FRAGARIA VIRIDIS

The third wild strawberry in Europe was *Fragaria viridis*, which was once widely cultivated on the Continent for its flavour and scent. It is a coarse, tiny berry, and among all the strawberries it is the species most tolerant of lime.

ALPINES

The autumn-fruiting varieties related to *Fragaria vesca* are popularly known as 'alpines'. These plants are native to high altitudes. While they are known to have been in garden cultivation in about 1530, little attention was paid to them until 1764, when a certain M. de Fougeron brought back a strain of alpine which he had found growing on Mont Cenis. These strawberries – with larger fruit and a longer, later cropping season than their cousins from the woods – found immediate favour with the French.

A few years earlier, in 1760, George II of England had received some alpine seeds from Turin. George W. Johnson, writing in the *Gardeners' Monthly* in 1847, tells us: '. . . it was such a rarity that a pinch of the seed sold for a guinea, but its fecundity very speedily reduced this price'.

For a few years there was much traffic in alpines. The Dutch sent plants to England; and from England and Holland plants and seeds went to the French king's gardens in the Trianons at Versailles. William Cobbett recorded: 'I have recently discovered [1833] . . . that there is a sort of alpine strawberry which, perhaps, taken altogether, is the most valuable of the whole. The French call it the *Cisalpine strawberry*, or the Strawberry of Napoleon.' By 1847 the alpine seed was being imported to England from France, where the variety has remained popular to this day.

The history of the development of the alpine is obscure; but the varieties can be divided into two types: those with runners and those without.

In spite of new improved varieties of garden strawberry, the tiny alpines still continued to triumph by their taste and fragrance in the minds of many gardeners – and certainly most gourmets. But the pre-eminence of the alpine was not to last. The tremendous interest in horticulture, the rapid development of the new 'scientific method' and of the fascination for botanical classification, and the widespread rise of market gardening, accompanied by the population explosion of the cities and their need for fresh foods – all of these, towards the end of the eighteenth century, added momentum to the development of new varieties of strawberry at a pace that left the alpines far behind. The idea that 'big is beautiful' started long ago in our society and the strawberry has been only one of many things which have fallen prey to this unfortunate attitude.

'The greatest service which can be rendered
any country is to add a useful plant to its culture.'
Thomas Jefferson, 'Garden Book'
(ed. Edwin M. Betts, 1944)

STRAWBERRIES FROM THE NEW WORLD

In 1753 the Swedish naturalist Linnaeus (Carl von Linné) published his *Species plantarum*, in which he made use of his new system for classifying plants. At last the strawberries of Mount Ida, the domesticated wild berries recorded by Pliny and the culinary source of Cardinal Wolsey's delight could be identified and named on a logical and international basis. Linnaeus' taxonomy set the scene for the development of new varieties of strawberry, since the close relationship between the various similar, but nevertheless distinct, varieties of the plant could now be appreciated.

However, the strawberries we cultivate now had their origins not in the institutionalized research efforts of establishment science but in the fortitude of one man, assisted by a lucky accident. And the strawberries which were the ancestors of those we grow today came from the New World.

In seventeenth-century Europe the hautboy was the strawberry most widely favoured but also esteemed was the North American *Fragaria virginiana*, recorded as under cultivation in France by Vespasian Robin, botanist to Louis XIII of France, in 1624, and noted both by Tradescant in his catalogue of 1623 and by Parkinson five years later. This American variety was called the 'Scarlet' because it produced a bright crimson fruit –rather small, but sweet. It was commercially important in England and America from the seventeenth century until the middle of the nineteenth, when improved hybrids took its place.

Early travellers in America reported that in the prairies 'the strawberries grow so thick that the horses' fetlocks seemed covered with blood'. When the Pilgrim Fathers arrived in the 1620s they learned from the Indians how to gather and use wild foods, the most important being maize. One of the others was the wild strawberry: the Indians made a strawberry bread of ground maize and berries. By 1645 Roger Williams, among others, was writing about the medicinal properties of the strawberry and quoting English doctors to support his claims of its successful curative use among the American Indians. Some of these, the Dakota and the Menomini, who lived near the Great Lakes, called June the 'Strawberry Moon'. Wild strawberries continued to be abundant in America for many years.

The strawberry is mentioned by all the most important early American writers on plants and gardens. These include Cotton Mather (1663–1728), Governor John Winthrop (1588–1649), his son John Winthrop Junior (1606–1676), John Josselyn (*fl.* 1638–1675), Roger Williams (*c.* 1603–1683) and William Wood (*fl.* 1629–1635).

Thomas Jefferson (1743–1826) in his *Garden Book* for 1767, records that his strawberry plants in their first year bore twenty berries each and that it

*Strawberries appear frequently in 'The Garden of Earthly Delights'
by Hieronymus Bosch (c. 1450–1516)*

took a hundred to fill half a pint. (So greatly have strawberries increased in size that today it would take fifteen or even less to fill half a pint.) In writing about the flavour and quality of the new French strawberries from Fontainebleau, on 28th October, 1785, Jefferson remarked to the President of William and Mary College, Virginia, that these 'strawberries are fair, but I think lack flavour'. Later, writing to his daughter from New York in 1790, he asked whether the whippoorwill bird always arrived with strawberries in the garden; anything connected to the season's harvest was worthy of discussion.

Between 1776 and 1820 in his *Weather Memorandum Notes* Jefferson discusses the order of terraces in his garden and notes that these are arranged first with figs, then the walk, next the strawberries, and finally terraces of grape-vines.

There was much correspondence about strawberries between American gardening enthusiasts. Jefferson, when writing to James Monroe on 26th May, 1795, mentioned the few objects which he felt especially enriched his country: '. . . the alpine strawberry, the skylark and the red-legged partridge'. He added: 'I despair too much of the nightingale to add that.'

The native North American wood strawberry, *Fragaria virginiana*, had better colour and was bigger than the other native varieties, although it did not compare in flavour. The exact date of its introduction into Europe is not known, but, as I have noted, the records of Vespasian Robin, botanist to Louis XIII of France, show the variety was in the royal gardens in 1624. It is likely that John Tradescant Senior (died *c.* 1637), while seeking new plants for English gardens on the Continent, brought *Fragaria virginiana* to England.

Although this berry was cultivated for over a hundred years on both sides of the Atlantic, no horticultural improvements resulted – just as with the other native European strawberries such as *Fragaria vesca*. The ancestor of today's garden strawberry was the large-fruited berry of Chile and other areas of South America, *Fragaria chiloensis*.

The story of how this strawberry came to Europe is a romantic one. A French officer, Amédée François Frézier (1682–1773), sent as a spy to South America, found *Fragaria chiloensis* in cultivation by the natives at the foot of the Andes near Quito. That Frézier's name derives from *fraisier* ('strawberry plant') is a pleasing coincidence.

Frézier dug up some strawberry plants to take home. France was at war, however, and the sea journey therefore took six months. During the long voyage fresh water became ever more precious and he had to share his own meagre ration with the plants. When, in August 1712, the ship finally put into Marseilles, five plants had survived the journey. Two of these Frézier gave to a colleague from the ship who had spared some of his water ration for the strawberries.

Frézier's plants became the foundation stock of the Chilean strawberries growing around Marseilles; two of them were sent to the king's gardens in Paris and by 1727 their progeny reached England. Philip Miller, gardener to the Worshipful Company of Apothecaries at their botanic garden in Chelsea, London, recorded that these plants were obtained from George Clifford of Amsterdam. And John Hill, in his *History of Plants and Trees . . .* (1756) mentions 'the great fruited strawberry of Chile with fleshy leaves'.

EMERGENCE OF TODAY'S STRAWBERRY

In modern times when we accept, with little real understanding, an endless number of scientific claims as part of everyday life, it is not easy to conceive of a time when the basic facts about the reproduction of a plant as commonly grown as the strawberry were unknown – when, even more incredibly, they were not believed even after their discovery. Yet until late in the eighteenth century it was not known that varieties of the strawberry differed in their reproductive characteristics.

Some strawberries are fertile, having both male and female parts (stamens and pistils); these are described as 'perfect'. Some are 'imperfect', having one or other of the reproductive parts and requiring cross-fertilization. Some are simply sterile. (Although records of what happened when Frézier's plants reached the French royal gardeners in Paris are now lost, it is known that they were imperfect females.)

We owe the botanic discovery of the reproductive traits of the strawberry to a brilliant young Frenchman, Antoine Nicolas Duchesne. He was born in Versailles in October, 1747, and published a manual of botany in 1764 when he was just seventeen. The following year he observed that not all strawberries were perfect hermaphrodites (i.e., that not all plants were both female and male). It is likely that his curiosity was first aroused by the Chilean strawberry, for he says that its cultivation had been abandoned in his day because of its 'sterility' and that it was so scarce in France that only once had he tasted one. Nevertheless it was this variety, *Fragaria chiloensis*, that he chose as one of the two varieties for his crucial experiment. He cross-pollinated males of one kind with females of another.

There is some dispute as to whether the pollen he used came from hautboys or *Fragaria virginiana*. In any case he obtained hybrid plants which produced fruit of admirable beauty; Louis XV decided to grow them in the kitchen gardens at Versailles following Duchesne's method. From these early plants came the seeds which were to create a new race of strawberries, including the first large-fruited, cultivated variety, *Fragaria ananassa*, which found immediate public favour.

Although French gardeners wisely took Duchesne's point and practised cross-pollination, more than forty years were to pass before any application of his discovery was made outside France (much later, there was to be a controversy about it in America). It is remarkable that this important technique should not have been immediately adopted by non-French growers – particularly in England with the *Hautbois*, which planted alone achieves such poor fertilization that at one time growers thought the strain was 'growing weak', yields having diminished so much.

Duchesne systematically described strawberry species brought together from all over the Western world for breeding purposes. He published his *Histoire naturelle des fraisiers* in 1766, and expressed amazement that before himself there had been no historian of the strawberry. He was then nineteen years old. He records: 'In forest country they eat a lot of strawberries; the consumption at Compiègne when the court stays there is one of the most considerable. But to supply Paris it has been necessary to cultivate entire fields of strawberry plants.'

At the time of publication of Duchesne's history, the favourite market strawberry around Paris was the *capron*, or *chaperon*. Later to be called the 'Fressant Seedling' of *Fragaria vesca*, it had a large pale berry, and had been developed about 1660 at Montreuil. It is thought to have been the first cultivated strawberry variety and is the first improved strawberry seedling of which there is record.

Duchesne's name appears in the classification of many varieties of strawberry; his history remains an oft-quoted source of observation and botanical information. Hardly anyone who has written on the strawberry in the last two centuries fails to refer to him. He enjoyed a long life, dying in Paris in 1827 at the ripe old age of eighty.

His work, however, had been stopped by the Revolution, but his results were taken up before his death by botanists and horticulturalists in England. Michael Keens (c. 1762–1835), a market gardener in Isleworth, near London, worked with *Fragaria virginiana* and *F. chiloensis* to produce new varieties, such as 'Duke of Kent' and 'Carolina'. In 1806 he improved on these, producing 'Keens' Imperial'. From this plant came the parent of our modern strawberries, the sensational 'Keens' Seedling', outstanding for its size and flavour.

'Keens' Seedling' came into commercial cultivation in 1821 and quickly spread to the Continent and to America as early as 1829. In that year William Cobbett, in *The English Gardener*, said: 'The great strawberry now-a-days is that raised from seed by a Mr. Keen of Islington which is

'Wilmot's Superb Prolific'
by C. J. Robertson, 1824

therefore called *Keens Seedling.*' When Cobbett gathered some 'Kew Pine' and some of the new 'Keens' Seedling' and set them before his friends to taste, 'everyone thought the *Keens* the best'.

Michael Keens also maintained an avid interest in alpines. In a letter to the Royal Horticultural Society on 9th July, 1817, he recommended always planting alpines by seed in rows 2ft [60cm] apart with 12in [30cm] between plants, at the back of hedges or walls in rich and very moist soil. 'My alpines, this year, thus managed, are bearing most abundantly, so much so, that in gathering them there is not room for the women to set their feet, without destroying many.'

Thomas Andrew Knight (1759–1838) produced his share of the hybrids that have contributed to the modern strawberry. His best were called 'Downton', 'Elton Seedling' and 'Elton Pine'. When a specimen of 'Downton' was sent to the Royal Horticultural Society in July, 1818, Knight stated that 'the plant seems to possess a singular hardiness in its leaves, as they remained quite fresh and green through the whole of the two past winters'.

There were many other outstanding varieties developed in this great flurry of strawberry hybridization. Among them were the 'Roseberry' from Robert Davidson of Aberdeen (1810); 'Wilmot's Superb' (1825); W. Atkinson of London's 'Grove End Scarlet' (1820); and 'Myatt's Pine', 'Prince Albert', 'Eliza' and 'British Queen', all of which were bred in the early nineteenth century. Scotland was not left out: strawberries supplied lucrative employment, and 60,000–80,000 pints of Scottish berries were sent to market every season.

By 1882, over two hundred sorts of strawberries had been developed in England. The modern strawberry had arrived in no uncertain fashion.

PINES

The word 'pine' appears frequently from the eighteenth century onwards. The pine is considered a variety of *Fragaria chiloensis* but its parentage and birthplace are uncertain; it was known to gardeners in England and France by the middle 1700s. While the first Chilean strawberries were tender and shy of bearing in the English climate, the pine variety was to have a powerful influence on the nineteenth-century development of new strawberry types.

The pine was known also as the 'Carolina' and the 'Old Pine'. James Barnet, reading a paper entitled 'Account and Description of Varieties of Strawberries' at the Horticultural Society of London on 7th December, 1824, remarked rather tetchily: 'It is somewhat singular that a strawberry so generally known, and of such excellence should have been confounded under such a variety of names.' He then proceeded to list twenty-one synonyms for the 'Old Pine' alone.

How did the term 'pine' arise in the first place? Some claim that it sprang from describing a taste so very different from that of the wood strawberry; others think it arose because the shape was like that of a pine-cone or of a pineapple. Some refer to the tradition of 'forcing' early strawberries in hothouses (or stoves) where pineapples were also grown. The horticultural historian U.P. Hedrick says in his *Cyclopedia of Hardy Fruits* (1922) that the name refers to the berry's pineapple fragrance. And, just to confuse the whole issue, strawberries of the species *Fragaria viridis* were often called 'Pine-Apples' because of their rich flavour. These are muddy waters for the strawberry historian.

OUT OF SEASON

Possibly the most eminent gardener in mid-Victorian times was Sir Joseph Paxton (1801–1865). Among his many accomplishments were his mastery and popularization of the use of the heated greenhouse. The professional growers seized upon this new tool and strawberries, among other produce, were 'forced' to come to the market early and out of season.

Theorem painting – an example of American Folk Art

People with more money than sense – or apparently taste – have always been prepared to pay extravagant prices to enjoy strawberries when other people cannot. Even the Romans had 'forcing houses' in the time of Pliny and these are mentioned by Martial. Today it is possible in Britain and America to buy strawberries the whole year round. They come from wherever in the globe that mild summer weather is to be found. Fashionable restaurants in London offer strawberries throughout the year, many of which have been shipped before the sun has sugared their juices and deepened their colour. They are hard, unsweet and desperately sad.

Nicholas Longworth

THE AMERICAN SCENE

While growers in Britain were seeking further improvements using variations of 'Keens' Seedling', the Americans joined the chase. Nicholas Longworth (1782–1863) and Charles Mason Hovey (1810–1887) are the most interesting and important of the American horticulturalists of those times.

Longworth, a self-made millionaire, retired early and devoted himself to gardening. After grapes he was fondest of strawberries – but at first he was unsuccessful with them. It was pure chance which allowed his eventual success.

Near Cincinnati there was a German called Abergust who knew how to grow strawberries. One day his son visited Longworth and told him not to expect many strawberries from his crop because all his plants were self-sterile. This remark provoked Longworth to start a study of strawberry blossoms. He concluded that 'imperfect' and 'perfect' flowered varieties had to be interplanted with each other for successful culture. He first published his findings in 1834 and then, in 1842, precipitated the 'Strawberry War' with his claims. This argument lasted in America for nearly two decades and involved most of America's foremost horticulturalists – who opposed Longworth's theories.

Duchesne's discovery, it seems, had been forgotten. Although Keens had applied it, new strawberry varieties descended from the pines had driven the hautboys and the original Chiles from English gardens and with them had gone British pollination problems. The difficulties were simply forgotten as the old varieties were dug up and the new ones planted. Eventually most English horticulturalists – including John Lindley in 1863 – even came to disbelieve in the existence of a separation of sexes in the strawberry plant.

The British could afford to ignore the question but for the Americans pollination remained a real problem. The strawberry there became known as a 'fickle fruit' because of its failure to bear.

The controversy over Longworth's theory raged with much heat from 1842 to 1855. He and the loyal Cincinnati Horticultural Society stood against virtually all the other American horticulturalists, including Hovey. The three propositions at the heart of the 'Strawberry War' were:

1 Are there pistillate varieties that must be planted near pollen-bearing sorts in order to be fruitful?
2 Can the sex of a variety be changed from staminate to pistillate by culture?
3 Are pistillate varieties more productive and valuable than staminate sorts?

The first of these propositions was the correct one.

Longworth was able to point out that, within ten years of starting to put his theory into practice, Cincinnati had the best strawberry production in America. For a long time he maintained that, without exception, two forms of strawberry had to be interplanted, and he refused to accept the value of bisexual species. Eventually he admitted that in this respect he was wrong and developed the bisexual 'Longworth Prolific'. His work contributed considerably to the advancement of the strawberry industry in North America.

Although varieties of the pine had been imported in 1804, and became significant as the parents of hundreds of varieties developed in America, horticulturalists there for some years devoted greater attention to the development of the native *Fragaria virginiana*, importing what they called the 'Large Scarlet Chile' from South America in 1820. This

Charles Mason Hovey

assortment of varieties, each with a differing type of fertilization problem, coupled with the Americans' long argument over the strawberries' varied reproductive capabilities, led to confusion, and for a long time little real progress was made. By 1825 there were some thirty named varieties of strawberry under cultivation in America but none were of any great value. All were eventually replaced in 1838 when 'Hovey's Seedling' was introduced. This was the first American-cultivated strawberry variety to be originated by deliberate cross-fertilization.

'Hovey's Seedling' was an outstanding strawberry with 'dark rich shining red' berries. Its originator, Charles Mason Hovey, was a Boston horticulturalist, writer and editor who collected every variety of strawberry as soon as he learned of its existence. When in about 1829 he added 'Keens' Seedling' and 'Wilmot's Superb' from England to his collection, he expected 'that they would so far excell all others, as to discard the large proportion of them from cultivation'. However, he was to be disappointed: the summer heat and winter cold of America proved too fierce for his new arrivals and he failed to harvest a crop.

In the summer of 1832 he decided to try to develop his own plant. The following year he gathered seed from his best strawberries and in spring, 1834, he potted these up in his greenhouse. By 1836 the plants had come into full bearing. Hovey carefully selected the very best plant from the bed; he called it the 'Seedling' because its fruits were so exceptional. From the 'Seedling' he produced twelve runners which he set out in a new bed. Six years after his first attempt to find a better strawberry he was successful. He wrote in 1838 that: 'It produced one of the most remarkable crops of remarkable strawberries we ever saw.' That year he exhibited the 'Seedling' at the Massachusetts Horticultural Society, where the judges deemed it a 'perfect strawberry'. In the Boston market in 1840 plants of the 'Seedling' were sold at $5 per dozen and the berries at 50 cents a quart – in both cases double the respective prices of any other strawberry variety. The great size and good taste of this berry made it a favourite for local shows and editorial comment.

When a gardener called Cunningham showed a basket of 'Hovey's Seedling' strawberries at the Farmers' Club of New York in 1851, Hovey claimed that his variety produced the 'largest strawberry of any kind ever grown'. Cunningham's prize specimen was a single berry $8\frac{3}{8}$ inches [21cm] around. With some amusement Hovey wrote that this 'sustains the

'Hovey's Seedling'

character of Hovey's Seedling strawberry'. But this size record was to be broken in 1878 by the 'Great American', originated by E. W. Durand of New Jersey. 'The past season a specimen was measured by the officers of the New York State Horticultural Society that proved 14½ inches [37cm] in circumference and nearly 5 inches [13cm] in diameter.'

In spring 1838 Hovey selected a few varieties from his beds, let these crop in the summer of 1839 and selected the three finest plants. Two years later the plants had formed a fairly big bed and produced a good crop of fruit. He selected just one plant which, he said, 'from its earliness, size, beauty, exquisite flavour, abundant product and hardiness appeared distinct from any kind in cultivation'. He called it the 'Boston Pine'. It was a pale scarlet berry with juicy fruit and a fine flavour, and it measured 4–4½ inches [10–11cm] in circumference.

Later Hovey was to claim that, before his 'Boston Pine', there had been not a single American strawberry of real merit. Additionally, although he kept excellent journals of his work, he stated in *The Fruits of America* (1847–1856) and in his *Magazine of Horticulture* that the true parentage of both his famous seedlings would never be known. He said that frost had effaced the writing on the identification labels on his original plants, and, therefore, he himself was unable to determine the parentage with any accuracy.

With the introduction of 'Hovey's Seedling' and the 'Boston Pine', thousands of enthusiastic amateur gardeners and professional nurserymen in America set about raising new plants. Newspapers and journals eagerly sought to cater for this growing band. The seeds and plants they offered greatly speeded the development of new varieties and popularized gardening as a pastime. The money to be made in this way was not inconsequential. For example, some 300,000 plants of Andrew S. Fuller's 'Brookland Scarlet' – which had been raised from seed in 1859 and had long been a standard strawberry – were sent out by the *New York Tribune*.

In the southern states strawberries became a profitable commercial crop during the nineteenth century. The extension of railroad lines and, in 1838, the introduction of Morse Code, which assisted the control of marketing demand and supply, were important factors in the extension of commercial planting. During the 1850s the Tidewater region of Virginia was one of the high-production areas. Strawberries were carried by boat from the Virginian ports to the cities of the North, where they were sold for as much as $1 per quart. In those days $1 could be a man's weekly wage. By the time the American Civil War stopped this trade, Tidewater was shipping six million pints of strawberries *each year* from Norfolk, Virginia.

There does not appear to have been a commercial strawberry industry outside the South until after 1860 but the retail trade sold all the fruit it could lay its hands on. In 1861 the *New York Times* reported: 'The strawberry trade of New York is the largest of any one point in the world . . . New York City received last year from all sources not less than 8,000,000 baskets of strawberries.'

After the war the market boomed again and by 1880 there were so many strawberries coming from the South that northern growers were struggling to stay in business. Within thirty years southern berries were

World's largest strawberry, Conway, Mass.

955

appearing in the Boston markets as early as January and flooding northern markets in March and April, fully two months before the local crops were ripe.

This dominance of the southern states was not to last, however, for American investors developed Mexico as a huge strawberry-producing region. Ernest Feder, in *Strawberry Imperialism* (1977), says: 'An initial reason . . . was that Mexico is able to produce *fresh* strawberries at a time when U.S. production is at a seasonal low. As a practical necessity, however, the production and marketing of fresh strawberries expanded quickly to encompass frozen strawberries . . .'

Refrigerated railcars came into wide use around 1880. The pioneer of strawberry refrigeration was Parker Earle of Cobden, Illinois. From his own account:

'I got a car from Michigan Central Railway that was being built to carry dairy products . . . I went ahead to Detroit to make sure of a market, and the car was loaded by the growers . . . it might have gone through in fair condition, but for the misfortune that some wise railroad man took out the plugs from the ice boxes in the roof to give the berries "a chance for a little air", and left them out. Of course, the ice was melted in a day and the bulk of the cargo was ruined . . . I went to Chicago and engaged the best refrigerator car then made, the old Tiffany . . . I built a cooling house at Anna [Illinois] large enough to hold ten tons of s'berries, and I cooled the load down for a day in that house, then transferred it to the Tiffany car . . . The result was a complete success from the start. No such solid, good-keeping berries had ever been seen in Chicago . . . From this time forward the evolution in transportation methods was accomplished.'

This claim was not an exaggeration. The strawberry trains coming through Illinois six years later consisted of 'thirty refrigerator cars per day, twenty-two of which go to commission men of Chicago whose 800,000 inhabitants consume 435,800 quarts a day'. The South benefited from the technological advance too: new boats were fitted with refrigeration so that cargoes were increased from 600 to over 25,000 packages of berries a trip.

The great interest in strawberries proved profitable for horticultural

The 'Roseberry' or
'Rose Strawberry' by
W. Hooker, 1817

writers, one of the most successful being R. G. Pardee of Palmyra, New York, whose *A Complete Manual for the Cultivation of the Strawberry*, first published in 1854, ran into eight editions.

Many of the claims made for new varieties of strawberry went beyond matters of mere taste and size. The 'Colfax', introduced in 1867, was said to 'kill weeds and everything else and completely occupy the ground'. The 'Necked Pine' was recommended as 'death on blue grass; it will jump over the fence and escape everything that trespasses. Plant it thirty feet apart and let it run.'

From an insignificant start at the beginning of the nineteenth century, the strawberry became, within sixty years, a major garden plant in America. It has received more attention from American plant breeders and enthusiasts than any other fruit except the grape. When U. P. Hedrick published his *The Small Fruits of New York* in 1926 he described 1,362 varieties of strawberry: almost every one of them had originated in America.

THE STRAWBERRY OF TODAY

After these American developments, England provided the next major improvement, a success which is generally agreed to have been unequalled until the last few years. Thomas Laxton (1830–1890), who had begun work on strawberries in 1878, producing the 'Noble' and 'King of Earlies', crowned his efforts in 1892 with a deep red jewel of a berry, exquisitely flavoured and justly named the 'Royal Sovereign'.

At long last mankind had produced a strawberry that, if not better than *Fragaria vesca*, could at least be honourably offered up as the most princely of modern consorts to that ancient queen, the wild strawberry, about which William Butler (1535–1618) made his famous remark:'Doubtless God could have made a better berry, but doubtless God never did.'

Laxtons' 'Noble'

Laxtons' 'Royal Sovereign'

TWO

EATING THE STRAWBERRY

> Rawe crayme undecocted, eaten with strawberys
> or hurtes is a rural mannes banket. I have
> knowne such bankettes have put men in jeopardy
> of they lyves.
>
> *Andrew Boorde, 'Dyetary of Helth', c. 1542*

The first and the best way to eat strawberries is straight from the plant. Add nothing: simply pick them, brush away any soil and eat them. Their smell is bound to increase your enjoyment: it has inspired poets no less than gourmets. The modern French historian, Fernand Braudel, rightly claims that 'the mere smell of cooking can evoke a whole civilisation' – and the strawberry, among all the fresh foods, has long been a trigger for memory as well as appetite.

Until quite recently fresh berries were to be had only in season, from about June to October. Nowadays cheaper air-freight has brought year-round availability. In America, not only has the country different climates in different regions, so that the season is 'extended', it is also supplied from Mexico.

No doubt many people feel that this year-round convenience is a good thing, but to every thing there is a season, not least man, and I enjoy looking forward to the taste of the summer's first strawberries. They always seem sweeter when they have ripened in the sun of your own country; and the fragrance brings simultaneously a nostalgia for forgotten summers and the excitement of one just beginning.

38

'Strawberries and Gooseberries on a Stone Ledge' by Adriaen Coorte, 1696

Thomas Jefferson, like so many other people during the eighteenth and nineteenth centuries, recorded in his garden diary the first strawberries and peas with a delight that did not diminish over the years. But Alice B. Toklas, that eccentric of the kitchen, felt moved to voice her disapproval of this habit in the French '. . . when in the strawberry season we were hospitably proffered by our hosts and hostesses strawberries – beautiful, luscious, fragrant, but strawberries, strawberries – twelve times in six consecutive days.'

The strawberry may be small but it packs an amazing dose of Vitamin C. It ranks with spinach and watercress, and is topped only by blackcurrants, rosehips and sprouts in the supply of this essential vitamin. There is, however, a significant difference in Vitamin C content between the various varieties and the level is affected also by the exposure to sunlight that the berries have had. The levels of other vitamins differ from variety to variety. Berries ripened on the plant, however, always have more vitamins than those ripened off.

In our long tradition of not leaving well enough alone we have managed to contrive a great many recipes for the strawberry. The great French chef Georges-Auguste Escoffier (1846–1935) offered forty-two different ways of serving them. It is the easiest of all fruits, save the apple, to combine with an almost infinite number of other ingredients. Some recipes are delicious, such as an uncooked purée of the berries poured over a mound of sweet fresh cream cheese, but others are a waste of both fruit and time, most especially those recipes from the years between the two world wars which advocated the inclusion of evaporated milk or artificially flavoured jellies. In almost all recipes the taste – if not the smell – of the strawberry manages to triumph over an often unnecessary culinary effort.

Besides being used fresh, there are three main categories of strawberry recipes and this has been so in the West for some 400 years: cooked for jams, jellies, sauces and pies; chilled or frozen for moulded desserts and ices; and distilled or mixed with wine and spirits. It is a fruit that can be eaten at any time or on any occasion. The Americans serve strawberries with whipped cream on hot waffles for breakfast. The French court of the seventeenth century liked them as a delicate frozen water. Extravagant romantics dip them one by one in champagne to feed a lover.

FRESH STRAWBERRIES

PURE ESSENCE OF ARABIAN NIGHTS

Alice B. Toklas included strawberries along with peaches, sugar, figs, Kirsch, cream and pistachio nuts in this romantically named dish.

Make a syrup by boiling together 8fl oz (225ml) water and 8oz (225g) sugar for 5 minutes. Pour boiling water over 6 peaches and peel them. Poach them in the syrup for 10 minutes. Drain and place in a serving dish. Blend 12 ripe figs and cook this purée for 10 minutes in the syrup in which the peaches were cooked. Add 2fl oz (55ml) of Kirsch to the cooled fig mixture, then cover the peaches with it. Decorate with hulled strawberries and chopped pistachios. Refrigerate for 1 hour. Serves 6. (1 cup water, 1 cup sugar, ¼ cup of kirsch)

STRAWBERRIES IN A SHALLOW DISH (FRAISES EN VASQUE)

The Toklas recipe is not as quaint as it may sound. Peaches are commonly used in combination with strawberries. Pistachio nuts – first brought, so it is said, to Rome from the Levant by Aulus Vitellius (AD 15–69) – have long been used as a flavouring. They are included in this dish which Narcissa Chamberlain in *The Flavour of France* (1960) claims for the area of Savoy.

Wash, drain and hull 2 lb (900g) strawberries. Washing strawberries before hulling is best – otherwise the water enters and softens the fruit. Put them in a shallow serving bowl, preferably of glass or undecorated white china. Sprinkle lightly with sugar and 2 tablespoons of cherry brandy. Chill for several hours. Cover tightly, for the smell of strawberries will invade other food in the refrigerator.
Just before serving, pour about 10fl oz (300ml) *crème fraîche* over them. Sprinkle with a handful of chopped pistachio nuts. Serves 6. (6½ cups strawberries, sugar, 2 tbs cherry brandy, 1¼ cups *crème fraîche*, ⅓ cup pistachio nuts)

Crème fraîche, which is developed deliberately to give it a very slightly acid taste, is sold throughout France. It is available in a number of speciality food shops in Britain and America. To get a better approximation than our bland pasteurised cream, use a combination of half sour cream and half double (heavy) cream.

When the strawberries are truly succulent from sunshine, such as those sold in the Midi in early June, I leave out the cherry brandy and sugar and do not bother with the chilling, proceeding directly on to the addition of the *crème fraîche* and the pistachios.

STRAWBERRIES AND CREAM

Cardinal Wolsey is credited with having made strawberries and cream fashionable when, in 1509, he served them at a great feast. No record exists as to how his cooks prepared what has since become a traditional dish, but here are three of the many different modern versions.

1 Hull the strawberries. Sprinkle with sugar and let stand for a few minutes. Serve cream in a separate jug, and let each guest pour as much over the serving of berries as he or she likes.

2 Fill a large bowl with thick cream. Hull and sugar the strawberries. Fold them into the cream and serve. Individual bowls can be prepared the same way. If your strawberries are very large, slice them first.

3 Carefully brush off any dirt from each strawberry. Arrange them unhulled on a white plate. Offer the plate of berries with a separate bowl of vanilla sugar and a jug of thick cream. Each guest should pick an unhulled berry, roll it about in the sugar, dip it into the cream and eat it, tossing aside the remaining hull.

Whichever way you serve them, strawberries soon disappear. In the twelve days of the Wimbledon tennis tournament, the spectators consume twelve tons of strawberries topped with 14,400 pints of cream.

FRESH STRAWBERRY VARIATIONS

Place strawberries in individual glasses or bowls. Then do any *one* of the following.

English Majolica strawberry basket and spoon, 1872

Add a syrup made by simmering for 10 minutes equal parts of orange juice and strawberry juice with a quarter as much sugar.
Cover with cold pineapple juice and sprinkle with icing (confectioners') sugar.
Sprinkle berries with lemon juice and icing (confectioners') sugar, then decorate with mint leaves.

SELF-GARNISHED BERRIES

One of the best ways to serve strawberries is with a sauce, or *coulis*, of their own juice. It intensifies the overall flavour and is useful if you are trying to cut down on cream.

Hull 1½ lb (675g) of strawberries. Reserve 1 lb (450g) of berries and chill: liquidize and sieve the remainder. Sweeten this purée with 3–4oz (75–100g) icing sugar, stirring until dissolved. Just before serving pour some of the purée over the whole berries and pass the rest separately. (5 cups strawberries, ⅔–1 cup confectioners' sugar)

CREAM CHEESES WITH WILD STRAWBERRIES
(LES CRÈMES AUX FRAISES DE BOIS)

Elizabeth David, in her *French Provincial Cooking* (1960), declares: '. . . in its extreme simplicity this sweet, native to Anjou and Saumur, is one of the most delicious in all French cookery'. Here is her recipe:

'For three or four people whip ½ pint fresh double cream until it is stiff. Fold in 2 egg whites beaten as for a soufflé. Have ready a square of fresh new muslin placed in a little mould pierced with holes.
Turn your cream into this and fold over the corners. Stand the mould on some sort of trivet or stand over a plate, so that the cream can drain. Leave in a cold larder until the next day. Turn out the cream on to a plate; cover it completely with fresh plain unwhipped cream. Serve with plenty of soft white sugar and in the season with strawberries, raspberries, or wild strawberries.' (300ml/1¼ cups heavy cream, 2 egg whites)

STRAWBERRY CAKES AND BREAD

AMERICAN STRAWBERRY SHORTCAKES

Down where the sun's 'most always shining,
Where poverty clouds have a silver lining,
Where there's chicken and cornbread with every dining,
That's where the South begins.

Henrietta Stanley Dull, 'Southern Cooking', 1928

As cornbread and hominy grits are traditional fare to the southern states of America, so strawberry shortcake is to the whole nation. Wild strawberries grew in profusion, and were part of the diets of the early colonies, so strawberry shortcake probably spread throughout America from the south. It is basically a rather coarse, not necessarily sweetened, baking-powder biscuit dough formed either in single biscuits or in one large 'cake'. These are split while they are still warm, strawberries put between the cut halves and on the top, and whipped cream generously heaped over the whole affair.

In recent years American shortcake has developed into a version of the finer English 'Victoria sponge', but a hot English scone, split, buttered, and filled and topped with strawberries and whipped double cream closely resembles the more old-fashioned American version and is delicious.

The ladies of America, no less than famous French chefs, each have their own 'best' recipe for strawberries. Here is how the ladies of the village of Warwick, New York State, tackled the matter in 1916:

'One cup powdered sugar creamed with one tablespoonful of butter, three eggs, one cup of flour (heaping), two tablespoonsful of cream, teaspoon baking powder (well rounded). Beat the yolks into the cream, butter and sugar, then cream, then the whites alternately with the flour. Bake in layers. When cold lay between the cakes and over the top nearly a quart of fresh ripe strawberries. Sprinkle each layer and the top with powdered sugar. Eat with cream.'
(8oz (225g) caster sugar, ½oz (15g) butter, 3 medium eggs, 8oz (225g) flour, 2 tbs cream, 1 tsp (rounded) baking powder. 1½ lb (675g) strawberries, icing sugar for sprinkling. Bake in 8in (20cm) tins for about 20 minutes at 190°C (375°F) Gas 5)

AN ENGLISH SHORTCAKE OF 1887

'Place a shortcake in a glass dish. Mash some fresh strawberries in a bowl, sweeten to taste, cover the shortcake with them, lay another shortcake on the top, and cover with cream either "whipped" or plain as liked. It should be made the day before it is required, so that the shortcakes may get thoroughly soaked with the strawberries and cream. It is a good plan to cut or break the shortcakes into pieces for the convenience of helping to the sweet.'

Mildred Blakelock, 'Old English Cookery, 1775–1931', 1932

GÉNOISE WITH ALPINE STRAWBERRIES

Recipes for strawberry shortcake can be successfully altered by changing the type of cake base and the strawberry filling. The French split a *brioche*, hollow it out, soak it in rum, and fill it with a mixture of strawberries and whipped cream.

For me, though, the best cake base is a génoise one. It is rich, moist and keeps well. Freezing several in advance makes the preparation of this dessert easy at short notice.

For the cake you will need:

2oz (50g) butter	4oz (100g) plain flour
6 medium eggs, beaten	a rectangular cake tin of 3 pint (1.7
8oz (225g) vanilla sugar	litre) capacity, about 13 × 4 × 3in
1 teaspoon vanilla essence	(30 × 10 × 7.5cm)

For the filling and icing you will need:

1½ lb (675g) cultivated alpine strawberries	5oz (140g) icing sugar
	½oz (15g) butter
4oz (100g) caster sugar	milk
1 pint (600ml) double cream	red food-colouring
1 tablespoon Cointreau	

Put to one side 14 strawberries and slice the rest into a bowl with the 4oz (100g) caster sugar. If you do not have enough alpine strawberries, make up the difference with ordinary ones sliced into small pieces. Preheat the oven to 180°C (350°F) Gas 4. Butter the cake tin and lightly flour it. Melt the butter but do not let it cool. Heat the beaten eggs in a double saucepan until they are just warm and then add two-thirds of the vanilla sugar and beat this mixture for 7 minutes. Slowly beat in the remaining vanilla sugar. Continue beating until the mixture turns a pale lemon colour and will stand in peaks. A large mixer makes light work of this and you do not need to beat it over hot water. Add the vanilla essence and fold in the flour, then the hot butter. Pour all this into the cake tin and bake for about 50 minutes or until done. Turn out onto a rack to cool.

When the cake is cold, split it lengthwise. Choose a flat rectangular dish, preferably of glass or white china. Whip the cream until stiff. Set the bottom half of the cake on the plate, sprinkle on the Cointreau, and spread the sliced strawberries over the top. Cover the berries with about an inch ($2\frac{1}{2}$cm) of the whipped cream.

Put on the other half of the cake and cover its top surface only with an icing made of the icing sugar, the melted butter and enough milk to make a smooth, firm mixture. Add a few drops of Cointreau and enough colouring to turn it a pale pink. (You can substitute strawberry juice for the water, Cointreau and colouring, but add it slowly or the mixture will become too fluid.) Now cover the sides of the cake with cream, reserving about half a cup. Decorate the top with lines of berry halves and pipe the remaining cream around the pink top and the base. Finish with a strawberry leaf at each end of the dish.

($\frac{1}{4}$ cup butter, 6 eggs, 1 cup sugar, 1 tsp vanilla essence, $1\frac{1}{8}$ cups sifted cake flour; $\frac{1}{2}$ cup superfine sugar, 6 cups alpine strawberries, $2\frac{1}{2}$ cups heavy cream, 1 tbs Cointreau, 1 cup confectioners' sugar, 1 tbs butter, milk)

STRAWBERRY BREAD

Strawberry bread was commonly used by the Indians in America. Roger Williams tells us in his *New England Journal* (1643) how they made it: 'The Indians bruise them in a mortar and mix them with meale and make s'berry bread.'

Any modern recipe for skillet or griddle cakes or for soda bread will serve as a basis for making this Indian bread if you use a proportion of $1\frac{1}{2}$ cups cornmeal to $\frac{1}{2}$ cup flour. Mash the strawberries before putting them in the mix. Do not add sugar to them.

STRAWBERRY PIES

Ask the average man what he prefers for dessert and almost invariably he will answer 'pie', says Henrietta Dull in her *Southern Cooking* (1928). She then adds, in those mannered days before women's lib: 'Women are not such pie eaters as men – but aren't most of us trying to please the men and give them what they want?' America still loves pies, even if a woman's place is no longer necessarily in the kitchen, and Mrs Dull had her favourite strawberry pie, named after a cousin whose preference it was.

WILLIE'S STRAWBERRY PIE

Halve and measure 1 cup of ripe strawberries. Put these into a baked pie shell. Crush and measure 1 cup of ripe strawberries, heat to boiling, add ½ cup sugar, 1 tablespoon cornflour and a few grains of salt. Cook 5 minutes. Cool and then pour over the berries in the pie shell. Put in refrigerator for 2 hours. Heap with whipped cream when ready to serve. This is a good pie to make with frozen strawberries. (6oz (175g) halved strawberries; 6oz (175g) crushed strawberries, 4oz (100g) sugar, 1 tbs cornflour, salt, 8in (20cm) cooked rich pie shell)

FRESH STRAWBERRY PIE

You will need 10fl oz (300ml) whipping cream. Blend 3oz (75g) cream cheese with 2–3 tablespoonsful of the cream to soften it. Spread this mixture over the bottom of a cooled, baked 9in (23cm) pie shell. Mash and sieve out the juice of 12oz (350g) of berries. Bring the juice to boiling point and slowly stir in 8oz (225g) sugar and then 1oz (25g) cornflour mixed with a little water. Cook slowly for about 10 minutes, stirring occasionally. Put another 12oz (350g) of strawberries in the pie shell and pour the mixture over them. Put pie in refrigerator until very cold. Decorate with the rest of the sweetened whipped cream before serving. (1¼ cups whipping cream, 6 tbs cream cheese with 2–3 tbs cream, 2½ cups strawberries plus 2½ cups mashed or sieved, 1 cup sugar, 2 tbs cornstarch)

QUICK STRAWBERRY PIE

Into a deep, rich baked pie crust put sufficient chilled and drained strawberries to fill it (about 1 lb (450g) for an 8in (20cm) crust) and cover them with sugar. Make a meringue of the whites of 2 eggs and 1 tablespoonful of sugar. Cover the pie with this mixture and brown quickly in a very hot oven. Serve immediately. The berries remain surprisingly fresh and uncooked.

THREE MISCELLANEOUS RECIPES

SARAH BERNHARDT STRAWBERRIES (FRAISES SARAH BERNHARDT)

'Madame Duchène asked Escoffier, "What is the real secret of your art? I have heard many explanations but I should like to learn the true solution of the problem from your own mouth." "Madam," replied Escoffier, smiling, "my success comes from the fact that my best dishes were created for ladies." Indeed, to modern eyes, a book of Escoffier's menus must be read like another charming ballad of the ladies of days gone by: Salade Rejane . . . mignonettes de cailles Rachel . . . poires Mary Carden . . . poulard Adelina Patti . . . coupe Yvette . . . fraises Sarah Bernhardt . . .'

Eugène Herbodeau and Paul Thalamas, 'Georges-Auguste Escoffier', 1955

Take some large strawberries, hull them, and soak them in Grand Marnier and sugar. Put some vanilla ice-cream with a thick pineapple purée into a serving dish. Arrange the strawberries on top and cover with a very cold – but not frozen – Curaçao mousse.

THE BENEFITS OF STRAWBERRY SYRUP

A bottle of strawberry syrup in the cupboard will earn its keep. It makes refreshing drinks, goes as a sauce over fruits and puddings, can be used in baking, icings and salads, and serves in or over creams, ice-creams and ices. Make it by combining equal weights of sugar and berries. Boil these until slightly thick. When cool, strain and pour into glass bottles.

STRAWBERRY SAUCE

This sauce can be used over a variety of sweets. It is good with most puddings – especially the little cream-cheese ones – and makes an outstanding addition to cakes and gâteaux in place of the traditional cream or icing.

To prepare the sauce, hull and wash with very cold water 1 lb (450g) of strawberries. Dry the berries and put them into a bowl. Pour over them a hot (but not boiling) syrup made from 8fl oz (225ml) water and 8oz (225g) sugar. Leave this mixture to cool and then strain through muslin. The resulting sauce should be decanted into a glass bottle, preferably with a glass stopper. (3 cups strawberries, 1 cup water, 1 cup sugar)

STRAWBERRIES WITH OTHER FRUIT

STRAWBERRIES WITH RASPBERRY PURÉE AND CRÈME DE CASSIS

Raspberries, strawberries and blackcurrants are the happiest of companions. Try this combination:

Hull 1½ lb (675g) strawberries. Put them in a shallow glass bowl and sprinkle lightly with sugar. Pour over them a purée made from 12fl oz (350ml) of sieved raspberries and 3fl oz (75ml) of crème de cassis. (5 cups strawberries, 1½ cups raspberry purée, ⅓ cup of crème de cassis)

STRAWBERRIES WITH LEMON

The French food scholar Dr de Pomiane, at lunch by the sea, served this strawberry dish in the wake of hot shrimps, curried mussels, skate, salad and cheese.

'I removed the stalks from 2 lb of strawberries, washed them in cold water and left them to drip. I squeezed the juice from a lemon and put it on one side. With a sharp knife I stripped the pith from the skin and discarded it. I was now left with the aromatic yellow skin of the lemon. This I cut into 10 or 12 pieces.

In a large bowl I mixed the rest of the lemon delicately with the strawberries and served them immediately.

I sat back and waited for coffee and Calvados. I did not have to wait for the compliments of my friends, I can assure you.'

Édouard de Pomiane, 'Cooking with Pomiane', 1962
(900g/6½ cups strawberries, 1 lemon)

FRUIT FILLED WITH STRAWBERRIES

Fresh oranges, pineapples and melons all combine well with strawberries. Scoop the pulp out of your chosen fruit and chop it into small pieces. Gently combine it with the strawberries and some sugar. Spoon this mixture back into the hollowed fruit shells. Chill before serving.

BERRY SOUP

If you like fruit soups you will find that strawberries and raspberries combine well. All you have to do is to take the raspberries, add sugar to taste plus some water and simmer. Then sieve the whole, add strawberry purée and a little arrowroot for thickening purposes, and boil gently for 5 minutes. Serve hot or cold. You can add some claret if you like, or cream or yoghourt – but in these latter cases make sure you do not reboil the soup.

PEARS WITH STRAWBERRY PURÉE

Peel 6 ripe, medium-sized pears. Poach in a little water flavoured with vanilla sugar. Leave them to cool in their syrup. Strain well, and place the pears in a serving dish and cover with a strawberry purée flavoured with sugar and 2 teaspoonsful each of Kirsch and maraschino cherry juice.

Peaches, especially white ones, and nectarines can be used with equal success in this recipe.

FRUIT IN A SHIRT (FRUIT EN CHEMISE)

Eliza Acton in her *Modern Cookery*, first published in 1845 and fortunately still in print, gives the following recipe for combining strawberries with an assortment of other fruits. Hulls and stems should of course be left on.

'Select for this dish very fine bunches of red and white currants, large ripe cherries, and gooseberries of different colours, and strawberries or raspberries very freshly gathered. Beat up the white of an egg with about half as much cold water, dip the fruit into this mixture, drain it on a sieve for an instant, and then roll it in fine sifted sugar till it is covered in every part, give it a gentle shake, and lay it on sheets of white paper to dry. It will dry gradually in a warm room, or a sunny window, in the course of three or four hours.'

COMPOTES, JAMS AND JELLIES

There is no 'best' recipe for strawberry jam – every cook has a favourite one – but a jam in which the berries are as whole as possible is preferable. Unless absolutely necessary, do not wash the berries before use, and, if possible, pick them on a dry day.

There are two approaches to the making of strawberry jams. One is to prepare the water and sugar as a syrup to receive the fruits; the other is to sugar the berries and let them stand for anything from three hours to overnight before cooking – this, it is claimed, firms the berries and helps to prevent them disintegrating during cooking.

Jams and jellies 'set' because of a chemical reaction between the pectin in the fruit and the sugar added to the mixture. Some fruits – apples and gooseberries, for example – have a high pectin content, but that of strawberries is relatively low. Pectin, which occurs in the cell walls of strawberries, has to be broken down at least a little before it is brought into solution. Some varieties are very low in pectin, so it may be necessary to increase it by adding ½ pint (300ml; 1¼ cups) gooseberry or redcurrant juice or the juice of several lemons to each 4 lb (1.8kg; 13 cups) of berries. A small amount of commercially prepared fruit-pectin or of citric or tartaric acid may be used in the ratio of ¼oz (1.8g) to 4 lb of berries. Even a teaspoonful of wine vinegar can be used. Do not add the extra fruit juice until towards the end of the cooking to make sure that it is not cooked too long, as otherwise it may substantially alter the flavour.

Keep the quantity of berries cooked at any one time to 4 lb or less. Preserving is better if done in small batches.

RED RED STRAWBERRY JAM

'Gather 2 pints perfect strawberries. Put them in a 10-inch [25-cm] very heavy cooking pot, cutting into a few of the berries to release a little juice. Cover with 4 cups sugar. Stir the mixture very gently with a wooden spoon over low heat until it has "juiced up". Then raise the heat to moderate and stop stirring. When the whole is a bubbling mass, set your timer for exactly 15 minutes (17, if the berries are very ripe). From this point do not disturb. You may take a wooden spoon and streak it slowly through the bottom to make sure there is no sticking. When the timer rings, tilt the pot. You should see in the liquid at the bottom a tendency to set. Slide the pot off the heat. Allow berries to cool uncovered. Sprinkle surface with juice of ½ lemon. When cool, stir the berries lightly and place in sterile jars.'

Irma S. Rombauer, 'The Joy of Cooking', 1936
(1½ lb/675g strawberries to 2 lb/900g sugar)

MIDDLE EAST STRAWBERRY JAM

The further east from England, the more often lemon is the fruit of choice to set strawberry jams and jellies. Claudia Roden, in *A Book of Middle Eastern Food* (1968), says '. . . jams remind me vividly of my childhood, of visiting relatives, of sitting on low sofas surrounded with bright silk cushions, of being enveloped by perfumes, faint and delicate or rich and overpowering'.

'Hull 2 lb (900g) strawberries, preferably wild ones. Layer strawberries and 2 lb (900g) sugar in a large glass or earthenware bowl, or in a deep china dish. Leave them to macerate for 12 hours or overnight. Transfer the strawberries and their juice to a large pan and add a little lemon juice if you like. Bring to the boil very slowly, stirring gently with a wooden spoon or shaking the pan lightly, and skimming off the white froth as it rises to the surface. Simmer for 10 to 15 minutes, depending on the ripeness of the fruit. Wild strawberries will require only 5 minutes,

sometimes even less. When the strawberries are soft, lift them out gently with a flat, perforated spoon and pack them into cleaned, heated glass jars. Let the syrup simmer for a little while longer until it has thickened enough to coat the back of a spoon or sets when tested on a cold plate. Pour over the strawberries and when cool, close the jars tightly as usual.'
(6½ cups strawberries (or 8 cups wild ones), 4 cups sugar)

The peel of 2 lemons, finely shredded, makes a good addition to this recipe, especially if put with the sugar and berries while they macerate.

Delicacy of taste and fragrance, as well as in size of serving, are features of Middle Eastern cookery. Mrs Roden suggests that jams such as this one are best eaten on their own, accompanied by a black coffee or a glass of cold water. This may sound too novel a custom – but why not try it? It treats the jam as a fine delicacy, gives rightful respect to good coffee-making, and focuses attention on the quality of the water.

WILD STRAWBERRY JAM

This jam is still made in Siberia where wild strawberries abound, but in England nowadays it would be a rare treat.

Gather about 2 lb (900g) wild strawberries on a dry day. Their scent will rise above all other plants in the wood save the violets. Gently roll the berries in a cloth; put them on a plate and sprinkle with a little sugar. Leave them to rest for a few hours.

Cook 2 lb (900g) sugar with 1 pint (600ml) water until thick. Add the berries. When they come to the boil remove from the heat. When boiling stops put them back on again until boiling restarts. Do this three times. Then cook the mixture over a very low heat until it is a heavy syrup. Pour into pots and cover when cool.

The jam will be thick and very rich. A spoonful over some cream cheese or in fresh home-made yoghourt is a blessing. (8 cups wild strawberries, 4 cups sugar, 2½ cups water)

COMPOTE OF STRAWBERRIES WITH ALMOND MILK

Elizabeth David adapted this recipe from one given in a book published in Turin in 1846. It was prepared by one Francesco Chapusat, who had been chef to the English ambassador to the court of Savoy.

Beatrix Potter illustration from 'The Tale of Johnny Town Mouse', 1918

'For 500g or 1 lb of strawberries, make the almond milk with 200g or 6oz of shelled almonds – preferably bought in their skins – 3 or 4 bitter almonds (or about 4 drops of pure extract of almonds), 200ml or just over ¼ pint of water. Sugar. Blanch the almonds, slip them out of their skins, put them to steep in cold water for a couple of hours. Pound them to a paste, adding a few drops of water, or rosewater if you have it, to prevent the almonds oiling. Mix very thoroughly with the water. (The blender can be used for these operations.) The mixture now has to be wrung twice through a finely woven cloth. This isn't really as daunting as it sounds but it does take a little time. What should – and does – eventually emerge is a smooth white milk. The residue of almonds is kept for some other dish. Almonds are far too expensive to waste. (A saving can be made – a saving of time, too – by simply stirring a couple of tablespoonfuls of very finely ground almonds into half a pint of thin cream. Leave an hour or two and strain.) Hull the strawberries. Arrange them in a glass or white china compote dish or bowl (or, perhaps easier to serve, individual goblets or bowls), strew them with sugar. Just before serving – on no account in advance – pour the almond milk over and round the fruit.' (3 cups strawberries, 1 cup shelled almonds, 3–4 bitter almonds or 4 drops pure extract of almonds, ⅔ cup water)

STRAWBERRY PRESERVES

Let 1¼ lb (550g) of berries and 1½ lb (675g) of sugar stand together for an hour. Put in a pot and boil until the sugar is dissolved. Cook for 3 but not more than 5 minutes. Let the mixture stand overnight. The next day, boil for 1 minute. Put the lid on the pot and let it rest for 2 minutes before stirring the mixture and pouring it into hot, sterilized jars. Seal while hot. (4 cups strawberries, 3 cups sugar)

USING PINEAPPLE OR RHUBARB IN STRAWBERRY PRESERVES

If you add any other fruit to strawberries you should let the mixture stand for at least 12 hours before first cooking. Pineapple and rhubarb each combine well with strawberries in a preserve. With pineapple, use a ratio of 8oz (225g) pineapple to 1½ lb (675g) berries and 1 lb (450g) sugar. If you use drained, tinned crushed pineapple, which I think works best, reduce the quantity of sugar by one-third.

With rhubarb, cut the rhubarb into tiny pieces and use a ratio of 5oz (150g) chopped rhubarb to 12oz (350g) berries and 1 lb (450g) sugar. Add some finely shredded lemon peel. (1 cup pineapple to 5 cups berries to 2 cups sugar; ¾ cup rhubarb to 2½ cups berries to 2 cups sugar)

RHUBARB AND STRAWBERRY CONSERVE

This American method from the 1930s works best if the ingredients are put together one morning and cooked the next.

Combine 10oz (275g) diced rhubarb, 6oz (175g) seedless raisins, the pulp and the grated rind from 2 oranges, and 1½ lb (675g) sugar. Let stand overnight.

Add 1¼ lb (550g) whole strawberries and cook until thick. Stir in 3oz (75g) chopped walnuts before potting. (The walnuts will cause the conserve to darken. To help avoid this, blanch the nuts in boiling water for a few minutes, then cool them in cold water and drain before using. (2 cups rhubarb, 1 cup seedless raisins, 2 oranges, 3 cups sugar, 4 cups strawberries, ½ cup chopped walnuts)

TO PRESERVE STRAWBERRIES WHOLE

To every 1 lb (450g) berries allow 1½ lb (675g) sugar and 1 pint (600ml) redcurrant juice.

'Choose the strawberries not too ripe, of a fine large sort and of good colour. Pick off the stalks, lay the strawberries in a dish, and sprinkle over them half the quantity of sugar, which must be finely pounded. Shake the dish gently, that the sugar may be equally distributed and touch the under-side of the fruit, and let it remain for 1 day. Then have ready the currant-juice, boil it with the remainder of the sugar until it forms a thin syrup, and in this simmer the strawberries and sugar, until the whole is sufficiently jellied. Great care must be taken not to stir the fruit roughly, as it should be preserved as whole as possible. Strawberries prepared in this manner are very good served in glasses and mixed with thin cream.'

Isabella Beeton, 'The Book of Household Management', 1862

(To every 3 cups berries, 3 cups superfine sugar and 2½ cups redcurrant juice)

————

'So enormous is the demand for strawberry jam that some of the great London houses convert from 50–100 tons of fresh strawberries into jam per day.'

David T. Fish, 'The Raspberry and Strawberry', 1882

————

STRAWBERRY JELLIES

While thick jam is best piled on muffins, buns or hot scones at teatime, strawberry jelly is, like quince jelly, delicate, and deserves to be eaten spread thinly on toast in the morning when the palate is fresh.

Here are three jelly recipes, each of which will give a good but different result. In the first recipe Miss Acton is referring to the immediate descendants of the American strawberry, *Fragaria virginiana*, which were known in her day as 'scarlets'.

1 'Take the small scarlet variety of strawberry, put some in an earthen jar, and stand the jar in a pan of boiling water. Let steam 3 or 4 hours, the water always boiling. When the berries are quite soft pour them into a sieve, or a muslin and strain out the juice. Allow 1 lb of white sugar to

each pint of juice. Boil the mixture until it thickens, which takes 30 or 40 minutes. The jelly must be made at once, that is to say as soon as the strawberries are strained, as the juice does not jell after it has once cooled.'

Eliza Acton, 'Modern Cookery', 1845
(450g/2 cups sugar to 575ml/2½ cups juice)

2 'Express the juice from the fresh fruit through a cloth, strain it clear, weigh, and stir into it an equal proportion of the finest sugar, dried and reduced to powder; when this is dissolved, place the preserving-pan over a very clear fire, and stir the jelly often until it boils; clear it carefully from scum, and boil it quickly from fifteen to twenty-five minutes.'

Eliza Acton, 'Modern Cookery', 1845
(1 cup juice to 1 cup sugar)

3 'Use very dry strawberries. Remove their stalks and put them in an earthenware jar to heat in a pan of water until all the juice is extracted. Pour them into a sieve and strain them after this through a jelly bag. Weigh the juice and the basin (the weight of the basin must be taken first), and boil it very quickly for fifteen minutes, then take it off the fire and by degrees put in fourteen ounces of sugar for every pound of juice. Boil again quickly for another fifteen minutes, when it should be ready. The colour should be brilliant and the flavour excellent.'

Hilda W. W. Leyel, 'The Complete Jam Cupboard', 1925
(For every cup of juice, 400g/⅞ cup of sugar)

STRAWBERRIES WITH WINE AND LIQUEURS

Red and white wines and a variety of liqueurs, notably Kirsch and Cointreau, work well with strawberries. The basic method is to put clean berries in a dish or in individual glasses, sugar them, and sprinkle them with any one of the following: wine, Kirsch, cherry brandy, raspberry brandy, Kümmel or best cognac. While any wine will do, champagne, sherry, port and Marsala are all widely used but the fortified wines are very overpowering for strawberries. For a real treat, try Muscat de Beaumes de Venise.

STRAWBERRIES WITH CLARET

Clean and hull the strawberries, sprinkle them with caster (superfine) sugar and add a tablespoonful of good claret for each serving. Do not serve with cream.

STRAWBERRIES WITH COGNAC

Wash, dry and hull some strawberries and sprinkle them with sugar. Cover them in cream whipped up with a little cognac.

STRAWBERRIES ROMANOFF

Soak 1 lb (450g) of strawberries in the juice of an orange and 2 tablespoonsful of Curaçao. Spoon the strawberries into a glass dish and cover them with Chantilly cream. (3 cups strawberries)

STRAWBERRIES IN CHAMPAGNE

Gently toss some strawberries in icing (confectioners') sugar, place them in suitable wine glasses and chill. An hour before serving, top up the glasses with chilled champagne and keep refrigerated. Then eat the strawberries and drink the champagne.

STRAWBERRY AND RASPBERRY LIQUEUR

Line up the following ingredients:

1½ lb (675g) strawberries	a few coriander seeds
12oz (350g) raspberries	1¾ pints (1 litre) good
1 lb (450g) vanilla sugar	Armagnac brandy

Wash and hull the strawberries and put them into a deep bowl with the raspberries. Boil the sugar with a little water until a thin syrup results. Add the coriander seeds to this and, when the syrup is cool, pour it over the fruit. Leave to marinate for 4 hours. Let the fruit and syrup mixture drip through fine muslin into a bowl, so that you get a clear liquid. Mix this with the brandy and then bottle. The resulting liqueur will retain the full flavour of the fruit. (5 cups strawberries, 2 cups raspberries, 2 cups vanilla sugar, a few coriander seeds and 4½ cups Armagnac brandy)

STRAWBERRY WHITE WINE (VIN BLANC FRAISE)

As a change from cassis, put some strawberry syrup (see page 48) into a glass together with the juice of half a lemon, a bit of peel and some ice; then fill up to the top with chilled dry white wine. For a non-alcoholic drink, use soda water instead of wine and you will disagree with G. K. Chesterton's claim that 'Heaven sent us soda water as a torment for our crimes.'

A CORDIAL WATER OF SIR WALTER RALEIGH

'Take a Gallon of Strawberries, and put them into a pint of Aqua Vitae, let them stand so for four or five days, strain them gently out, and sweeten the water as you please with fine sugar; or else with perfume.'

> *A Queen's Delight: or, The Art of Preserving,*
> *Conserving and Candying: As also A right Knowledge*
> *of making Perfumes, and Distilling the most Excellent*
> *Waters. Never before Published'. Printed by R. Wood*
> *for Nath. Brooks, at the Angel in Cornhill, 1658*

*Strawberries in early advertisements and
present-day packaging*

STRAWBERRY WINES

STRAWBERRY WINE 1

'To make eighteen gallons combine cold soft water, seven gallons
cyder, six gallons strawberries, six gallons raw sugar, sixteen pounds
red tartar, in fine powder, three ounces, the peel and juice of two
lemons. Brandy, Two or Three quarts.'

P. P. Carnell, 'A Treatise on Family Wine Making', 1814
(32 cups sugar; other ingredients as above: dividing by ten or twenty
gives manageable proportions)

STRAWBERRY WINE 2

Take 8 lb (3.6kg) of strawberries and mash them. Pour on 1 gallon (4.5 litres) of cold water and stir well. Leave for 3 days and then strain through muslin. Add 3½ lb (1.6kg) sugar, stir and cover. Leave this for a week and then strain it into a container and cap it. After 10 days fermentation should be complete. Now add ½ pint (300ml) whisky and leave. This wine matures rapidly and may be bottled in 6 weeks and drunk almost at once. (7 cups sugar; 1¼ cups whisky; 26 cups strawberries)

> Strawberry water was popular in Duchesne's time,
> served in summer in cafés or with light meals. Duchesne
> gave a recipe, having 'got it from Monsieur Onfroy,
> the King's Distiller': 'Take 1 lb of really ripe strawberries
> and a quarter pound of currants. Put them
> all in a bowl. Crush them together. Put in a pint of fresh water
> and 8oz of sugar and leave to infuse for a half hour.
> Then heat until really clear and then chill.'

SALADS

STRAWBERRY SALAD

Use ripe fruit. Quarter 2 skinned peaches and 3 apricots and put them in a bowl with a handful of white grapes and another of strawberries and raspberries. Sprinkle with sugar. Make a purée by sieving 8oz (225g) of strawberries and adding 2oz (50g) sugar and a glass of white wine. Stir well and let rest for half an hour, and then pour over the fruit in the bowl. Throw on 3 or 4 small young mint leaves. (2 cups strawberries, ¼ cup sugar, ⅓ cup white wine)

SALAD ELONA

In Germany fresh strawberries are often served as a garnish to cold salmon and salmon mousse and this salad, from *Jane Grigson's Vegetable Book* (1978), makes an excellent accompaniment to such dishes as well as to cold salmon trout and chicken. I have used it with equal success with smoked mackerel and kipper pastes. I prefer to salt, sweat, rinse and dry the cucumber before making up the salad.

'Alternate circles of thinly sliced peeled cucumber with circles of hulled and halved large strawberries. Season with salt, plenty of black pepper, a pinch of sugar. Pour over two or three tablespoons of dry white wine, or white wine vinegar.'

PUDDINGS

SUMMER PUDDING

The whole idea of this pudding is to make it from whatever soft fruits are available – most often these will be a mixture of red-, white- and blackcurrants, strawberries and raspberries.

Slice some white bread and trim off the crusts. Line the bottom and sides of a mould with the bread. Leave no gaps. Stew the currants with a very little water and 4oz (110g) of sugar to every 1 lb (450g) of fruit until the juices are running. Mix the cooled currant mixture and the fresh berries, and then pour into the mould. Cut a piece of bread to serve as a lid and put a plate with a weight on top of the pudding.

Leave it for several hours or, better still, overnight. Turn out onto a flat plate. The juices should have soaked through the bread so that it is the same colour as the fruit mixture.

For a slightly smarter version of this pudding, use boudoir biscuits instead of bread. ($\frac{1}{2}$ cup sugar, $2\frac{3}{4}$ cups fruit)

WINTER PUDDING

A strawberry pudding may at first glance seem a waste of strawberries and anyway who wants suet pudding in summer? But it's a good use for frozen strawberries because the taste is strengthened by the jam and it brings a memory of summer to a cold winter's day.

To make a strawberry pudding, line a basin with sweet suet crust. Put aside sufficient for the lid. Combine 1 lb (450g) strawberries with 6oz (175g) strawberry jam. Put the mixture into the lined basin with the juice of 1 lemon. Cover with a lid of suet crust and seal at the edges. Cover with foil and steam gently for $1\frac{1}{2}$ to $1\frac{3}{4}$ hours. Serve with homemade custard sauce. (3 cups strawberries, with $\frac{1}{2}$ cup jam)

'The strawberry grows underneath the nettle,
And wholesome berries thrive and ripen best
Neighbour'd by fruit of baser quality.'
Shakespeare, 'Henry V,' Act I, Scene i

STRAWBERRY FRUIT ROLL

In the land of Mount Ararat where Noah's Ark is said to have landed after the flood, they make a strawberry sweet which stays in the sun until ready to eat. If you should find the summer especially hot and dry, try making this dish.

Line the bottom and sides of pan with a piece of foil. Bend the foil over the edges of the pan. Boil 10oz (275g) strawberries with $1\frac{1}{2}$oz (40g) sugar. Sieve the mixture. Cool, then pour into the pan, spreading the mixture evenly. Cover with fine muslin. Put the pan in full sun and bring it in at night. Do this every day until the surface of the mixture is firm to the touch and dry enough to peel away from the foil in one piece. Cut in very small squares, arrange on a plate, dust very lightly with icing sugar. Serve with coffee. (2 cups strawberries, 3½ tbs sugar, a little confectioners' sugar)

STRAWBERRIES FONDANT (FRAGALE AL FONDENTE)

This is another sweet to serve with coffee – but make only a few as they are very rich.

Prepare some fondant icing by cooking sugar to the 'soft ball' stage (115°C; 240°F). Add a little berry juice and a few drops of lemon. Pour the mixture onto a smooth surface and work it with a spoon until it is smooth and cool.
Select a few fine large strawberries; leave on their hulls and stems. Reheat the fondant in a double saucepan until it is just liquid enough to pour (do not overheat or it will become grainy). Take each berry and dip it by hand into the fondant until it is covered to just below the hull. Place the berries separately on waxed paper in a tray, and refrigerate.

You can get the berries to stand up erect, but it takes practice. Letting the fondant cool slightly between dipping the berries and putting them on the tray helps.

STRAWBERRY FRITTERS

Every French province has its own collection of names and recipes for fritters – *roussettes, oreillettes, bugnes* . . . Here is Brillat-Savarin's recipe for strawberry ones.

'Combine flour, two eggs, two tablespoonsful of Kirsch, four of water. Soak your strawberries in sugar to start the juice running. Cloak each in the fritter paste and drop in boiling oil.'

Jean-Anthelme Brillat-Savarin, 'Real French Cooking', 1856

JALOUSIE

In her *Mastering the Art of French Cooking* (1969) Julia Child calls this traditional French sweet a 'peekaboo' tart. It is easy to make.

'Emma Van Name' by an unknown American artist, c. 1795

Roll out a long rectangle of puff pastry, about ⅛in (3mm) thick. Spread strawberry jam on it, leaving a ¾in (2cm) border of pastry all around. Turn this border up and over onto the jam.

Roll out a second piece of pastry big enough to cover this base. Fold this piece in half lengthwise and cut slits in the pastry ¼in (6mm) apart to within ½in (1cm) of the edges. Open this flat again and wet the edges. Put it on top of the jam-covered base. Pinch together the top and bottom pastries.

Chill for half an hour before baking at 230°C (450°F) Gas 8 for 20 minutes, then lower the heat to 200°C (400°F) Gas 6 and continue baking until brown and the sides are all crisp. Here is an example of not judging a book by its cover for this tart can end up looking a mess but its taste and smell will have you begging for more.

FRESH FRUIT TART

Bake blind a tart shell. When cool, fill with crème pâtissière and on top of this put fresh, well-drained and hulled strawberries. Top with a redcurrant glaze and serve cold.

STRAWBERRY YOGHOURT

Our oversweet processed supermarket yoghourts in the West are a poor imitation of the real thing. Yoghourt is easy and inexpensive to make at home. When you have done so, put in some fresh sliced strawberries,

Limoges porcelain tea set, 1984

some jam in winter, or dilute with cold water adding some strawberry syrup (see page 48) to make a delectable drink.

STRAWBERRY SOUFFLÉ

This is a delightful treat and more to my liking than iced soufflés. If you have to be careful about your intake of cholesterol this is a good recipe because no egg yolks are used. You can substitute frozen strawberries but, if so, boil the syrup longer to take account of the extra water content.

Mix 8fl oz (225ml) strawberry purée – representing about 10–12oz (300–350g) berries, mashed and sieved – with 4oz (110g) sugar and boil gently for a few minutes until it just starts to thicken. Allow it to cool and then carefully but completely fold it into 6 very stiffly beaten egg whites. Turn into a 7in (18cm) soufflé dish and bake in a preheated oven at 160°C (325°F) Gas 3 for 10 minutes until it is slightly raised and the top is golden brown. Serve hot.

This soufflé can be eaten cold, although it should not be refrigerated; however, some juice will sink back to the bottom. (1 cup strawberry purée (equal to 2 cups berries), $\frac{1}{2}$ cup sugar)

STRAWBERRY ISLANDS

This recipe using strawberries makes a pretty variation of *Oeufs à la neige*, those little light meringues of egg-white patterned with caramel and floating in custard which the English call 'Snow Eggs' or 'Floating Islands'.

3 eggs	$\frac{1}{2}$ teaspoonful vanilla essence
1 pint (600ml) milk, or slightly more	12oz (350g) strawberries
4oz (100g) sugar	1oz (28g) icing sugar

Separate the eggs and whip the whites until very stiff. Then slowly add 2oz (50g; $\frac{1}{4}$ cup) sugar to make the meringue. Bring 15fl oz (400ml; 1$\frac{7}{8}$ cups) of the milk just to the boil and then simmer it gently. Take a heaped tablespoonful of the meringue and shape it with a knife; then put a dent in it with a teaspoon. Slide this little mound into the milk and poach for 4 minutes, turning it after 2 minutes. Remove with a perforated spoon and put it to drain on kitchen paper.

Repeat the process until all the meringue has been used up. The quantities given here should make 12 'islands'. With practice you can poach 3 at a time.

To make the custard, beat the egg yolks with 2 oz (50g; ¼ cup) sugar. Make up the remaining hot milk to 15fl oz (400ml; 1⅞ cups) again and pour this slowly onto the yolks, whisking all the time. Put the mixture into a double saucepan and heat until it just coats the back of a spoon – it will thicken slightly on cooling. Strain into a clean bowl and stir in the vanilla essence. Put this to cool and make a purée of 3–4oz (75–100g; ⅔ cup) sieved strawberries and 10z (28g; 2 tbs) icing sugar.

When the custard is cold pour it onto a large plate and float the 'islands' in it. Place 2 or 3 alpine strawberries in the hollow of each 'island' and dribble the purée onto the custard. If you wish, make a caramel by boiling 2oz (50g) sugar with 2fl oz (60ml; ¼ cup) water until just golden. As soon as the bubbles have subsided dribble this onto each 'island' around the strawberries. This recipe serves 4–6. (3 eggs, 2½ cups milk, ½ cup sugar, ½ tsp vanilla essence, 2½ cups strawberries, 2 tbs confectioners' sugar)

'Blessed be he that invented pudding, for it is a Manna
that hits the Palates of all Sortes of People.'
Misson de Valbourg, 'Mémoires et observations . . .', 1698

STRAWBERRY VINEGAR

The Victorians liked fine fruit vinegars and used a spoonful or so in a glass of water as a drink in summer, or at any time of the year as a tonic for people of delicate disposition.

Take fresh ripe fruit and put it into a glass jar. Top it up with white wine vinegar. Tie wax paper over the top and let it sit for 3–4 days. Then empty the jar into a jelly bag and let the liquid drip through. Put fresh strawberries in the jar, and pour this liquid over them.

Repeat this process twice more, leaving 3 days between each operation. Take the final liquid and make a thin syrup by boiling it with an equal amount of sugar. Skim it thoroughly before putting it into a hot, clean bottle. Cork tightly after a week and store in a cool place.

CHILLED AND FROZEN DISHES

EAU DE FRAISES

Frozen waters were known at the French court as early as 1660. I am grateful to Elizabeth David for sending me this recipe from the 1724 edition of François Massialot's *Nouvelle Instruction Pour Les confitures, Les liqueurs et Les fruits.*

'Take a pound of very ripe strawberries, and a quarter of redcurrants; put them in a bowl; crush them together; put to them a pint of fresh water and squeeze in the juice of a lemon; add eight ounces of sugar, and leave all to infuse for half an hour, and press it through a sleeve until it runs clear, and put it in an ice-pot to freeze.' (450g (3 cups) strawberries, 110g (⅔ cup) redcurrants, 600ml (2½ cups) fresh water, 225g (1 cup) sugar)

ICED STRAWBERRY SOUFFLÉ

This combination of meringue and whipped cream freezes without churning. It serves four and is very rich, so use small, straight-sided ramekins which hold about 3–4 fl oz (85–110 ml; under ½ cup). Tie a paper or foil collar around each dish and put it in the freezer until ready to use.

Sieve 8oz (225g) strawberries and flavour with 1 tablespoonful of lemon juice or Kirsch. Heat 3½ oz (100g) sugar with 2½fl oz (75ml) water until dissolved, and then boil to the 'soft ball' stage (115°C; 240°F). Beat 2 egg whites until stiff, then slowly pour in the hot sugar mixture, beating constantly until it is cool and very stiff. It takes considerable beating to stiffen the mixture so keep at it.
Fold in the strawberry purée with ¼ pint (150ml) whipped double cream. Divide between the ramekins and freeze until firm(2–3 hours).
If tightly covered, these keep well for up to 2 months. When you want to serve them, take out of the freezer and put in the refrigerator 45–60 minutes before bringing to table. The soufflés should be stiff and cold when served – but not hard. (1½ cups strawberries, 1 tbs lemon juice or Kirsch, 7 tbs sugar, 5 tbs water, ½ cup plus 2 tbs heavy cream)

STRAWBERRY ICE CREAM

There are many recipes for strawberry ice-cream. I like these three, but some experimentation – perhaps adding orange juice, or mint, or redcurrant sauce – will lead you to your own special ice-cream recipe.

'Mix the fruit-juice, strained and sweetened, in the proportion of a pound to a pint of whipt cream.'
Margaret Dods, 'The Cook and Housewife's Manual', 1826
(3 cups strawberries to 2½ cups whipped cream)

Neither of the following ice-creams freezes into a block, but are ready to serve when stiff but still creamy. Use less sugar in the first recipe if the fruit is exceptionally sweet from the sun or if you prefer a less sweet taste.

Beat 4 egg yolks and put them into a double saucepan. Add ½ pint (300ml) double cream. Cook slowly, stirring constantly until it thickens. Add ¼ lb (110g) caster sugar and 1 lb (450g) crushed strawberries and put in freezer. Stir after the first hour. (4 egg yolks, 1¼ cups heavy cream, ½ cup superfine sugar, 3 cups crushed strawberries)

Mix 8oz (225g) sugar and 2 pints (1.1 litres) double cream. Put the sweetened cream in the freezer. Mash 1½lb (675g) strawberries with 8oz (225g) sugar. Let stand for an hour. When the cream is beginning to freeze – say, an hour – add the berry mixture. Stir well and put to freeze. Stir once more after another hour. (1 cup sugar, 5 cups heavy cream, 5 cups berries and 1 cup sugar)

STRAWBERRY ICE

Make 1 pint (600ml) of strawberry purée representing about 1½lb (675g) of sieved strawberries. Mix this with 1 pint (600ml) of syrup made from 8oz (225g) sugar and 16fl oz (425ml) water. Add the juice of 1 lemon. Blend well and then freeze. Serve with a few *langue de chat* biscuits. To make a richer sweet, pour strawberry sauce (see page 48) over the ice. (2½ cups purée, 1 cup sugar, 2 cups water)

STRAWBERRY MOUSSE

Blend and sieve 1½lb (675g) strawberries. Sprinkle with 4oz (110g) sugar and let rest for an hour. Moisten 5 teaspoonsful gelatine with warm water and leave to soften, then add to the purée. When this begins to congeal, fold in 15fl oz (400ml) whipped double cream. Freeze.

(5 cups strawberries, ½ cup sugar, 5 tsp gelatine, 2 cups whipped cream)

CHARLOTTE AUX FRAISES

The talented young chef Raymond Blanc, who believes the goal of his cooking should be to make people happy, kindly gave me his recipe for 'Charlotte aux Fraises', which he serves at 'Le Manoir aux Quat Saisons' in Oxfordshire. The ingredients are sufficient for 10 servings.

For the bavarois cream:

8 leaves of gelatine soaked in tepid water so that they become supple and melt easily, or ½oz (15g) granules soaked in 2 teaspoonsful water
18fl oz (550ml) milk
2 vanilla pods

7oz (200g) caster sugar
8 egg yolks
18fl oz (550ml) whipping cream
14oz (400g) strawberries plus 3½oz (85g) caster sugar
a further 4oz (110g) of berries to decorate the inside of the cream

For lining the mould:

boudoir biscuits, soaked in a syrup made by boiling 7fl oz (200ml) water and 7oz (200g)
sugar with 2 teaspoonsful Kirsch added when the syrup has cooled

For the coulis (sauce):

7oz (200g) strawberries
7oz (200g) raspberries
a syrup made from 7oz (200g) sugar and 7fl oz (200ml) water

For serving:

10 fine strawberries with stalks on, a rectangular terrine or cake tin of 2½–3 pint (1.4–1.7 litres)
capacity, measuring approximately 12 × 4 × 3in (30 × 10 × 7.5cm)

(*Cream:* 2¼ cups milk, 2 vanilla pods, ⅞ cup superfine sugar, 8 egg yolks, 8 leaves or 6 tsp gelatine, 2¼ cups whipping cream, 3 cups strawberries plus 7 tbs sugar, another cup of berries to decorate the inside of the cream. *Mould:* Boudoir biscuits, ⅞ cup water, ⅞ cup sugar, 2 tsp Kirsch. *Coulis:* 1½ cups strawberries, 1 heaped cup raspberries, ⅞ cup sugar, ⅞ cup water)

Line the mould with the boudoir biscuits soaked in the Kirsch syrup. Make the vanilla cream by boiling the milk with the split vanilla pods. Cream the sugar and egg yolks together in a bowl and pour the hot milk slowly over, whisking all the time. Pour the mixture into a clean saucepan, place over a low heat and stir constantly with a wooden spoon (if the temperature is too high the eggs will scramble and spoil the vanilla cream). Stir until the cream is just thickening, so that it coats the back of the spoon. Remove it from the heat and add the soaked gelatine leaves, which will melt very quickly. Stir and pass the cream through a fine strainer into a clean bowl.

Purée 14oz (400g) of strawberries with 3½oz (85g) caster sugar and pass through a fine sieve.

Whip the cream until it is just beginning to stiffen.

When the vanilla cream is almost cold stir in the strawberry purée and mix completely. Then fold in the whipped cream. This completes the first stage, the *bavarois* cream.

Pour half the *bavarois* cream into the lined mould and place a line of strawberries down the centre. Then pour the rest of the *bavarois* cream over this and trim the biscuits level. Put in the refrigerator for at least 1 hour. If covered this can be left for a day.

To make the *coulis* pass the 7oz (200g) of strawberries and 7oz (200g) of raspberries through a liquidizer and sieve. Make the syrup by boiling the 7oz (200g) sugar and 7fl oz (200g) water together. When this is cold, add the purée and a little lemon juice if necessary. There should be a hint of sharpness.

To serve, turn the charlotte out of the mould onto a serving dish and pour the *coulis* around it. Decorate the dish with a few whole strawberries, with their stalks on and rolled in caster sugar. Slice the charlotte and serve with some of the *coulis* around each slice.

FREEZING STRAWBERRIES

The popularity of 'pick-your-own' farms and renewed public interest in allotments and vegetable gardening provide many households with an abundance of strawberries for freezing.

Strawberries must be frozen at the peak of maturity: over-ripe soft fruit will give poor results when thawed.

A late 19th-century Royal Doulton dish

The problem with freezing strawberries is that they are almost 90 per cent water, so that when they freeze their cells are damaged by ice-crystal formation. This lets juice seep out of the damaged cells on thawing, so that the berries become mushy and lose their texture, shape and colour. The best mediums for freezing them are either dry sugar or, better, a syrup. The longer strawberries stay frozen, the greater the decrease in their flavour.

It is important to work quickly when freezing strawberries.

A cold 60 per cent sugar syrup is the best freezing medium, giving whole berries a better colour and improving the shape of thawed sliced berries. Hard water is better than soft for making the syrup, which should be chilled well before use to about 2°C (36°F). If you add 0.04 per cent citric acid the colour and appearance of the fruit should be improved for up to three months' storage; and the addition of 0.08 per cent ascorbic acid and 1 per cent calcium lactate will produce firmer fruit after six months' storage. Experiments have shown that berries in syrup quickly thawed under cold water show a better appearance, but thawing them slowly in the refrigerator does not affect quality.

When using dry sugar, open-freeze whole berries and then pack them in a single layer away from the pressure of other stored items. This will give the best appearance and colour to the thawed berries. Freezing them this way achieves a faster cooling rate, so there is less time for the sugar to draw out the juices of the fruit. One drawback of this method is that what looks like a white 'mould' forms on the berries during storage. This is made up of bits of sucrose hydrates which are harmless and disappear slowly during thawing.

Crushed or puréed berries should be mixed with sugar prior to freezing.

Frozen berries in any form will give poor results if used for jam because the already low level of available pectin has been reduced. If you have to make jam from frozen strawberries, add Bramley apples and use 20 per cent more berries than it says in the recipe you are following. The jam produced will be darker in colour and more sticky than set when cool. The recommended freezer life for strawberries is one year.

A STRAWBERRY FOOL

Strawberries are the most accommodating of fruit. Everyone has a favourite way with them.

A frequent guest at the Hôtel de Cap d'Antibes at the turn of the century was a 'strawberry fool'. Count Apraxine breakfasted regularly on a dozen fresh out-of-season strawberries, each of which cost a gold sovereign. He would carefully mash them to a pulp and return them to the kitchen uneaten.

What a shame – for the nicest thing of all about strawberries is that they are best eaten fresh from the plant. This makes for good eating and that, as the French chef Pellaprat pointed out, is 'one of the few joys of living that the cruel passage of time spares us'.

————

Curly locks, Curly locks,
Wilt thou be mine?
Thou shalt not wash dishes
Nor yet feed the swine.
But sit on a cushion
And sew a fine seam,
And feed upon strawberries,
Sugar and cream.

Infant Institutes 1797

THREE

Strawberries for Health and Beauty

The Lord hath created medicines out of the earth;
and he that is wise will not abhor them.
Ecclesiasticus

More than half of the four hundred herbs used by Hippocrates, the 'Father of Medicine', are still in use today. How these medicinal herbs came to be selected from those with no healing properties will probably remain a mystery forever: mankind most likely discovered them over millions of years by the slow process of trial and error. From the evidence of numerous fossilized seeds, it seems likely that the discovery of the medicinal properties of the wild strawberry was near the very beginning of the long search.

In the West today medical treatment usually starts with a prescription from the doctor which turns into a pill, capsule or liquid that we pop down our throats with the expectation of an instant cure. To most people such drugs seem unrelated to the flowers in our gardens or the fruit and vegetables on display in the supermarkets. Yet almost a third of all pharmaceutical products were originally derived from plants. How easily and quickly we have forgotten that the foxglove can provide a life-giving heart stimulant, or that the initial chemical for the contraceptive pill came from the wild barbasco root.

Our ancestors could not afford such lapses of memory. The curative properties of these powerful plants were passed by word of mouth and, later, through herbals from generation to generation. The subject of medicinal herbs stretches so far back in time that one seventeenth-century writer, William Coles, was moved to remark: 'It is a subject as ancient as the Creation, yea, more ancient than the sun or moon or stars, they being created on the fourth day, whereas plants were the third.'

Folk medicine exists in all parts of the world but the West owes its knowledge of herbal medicine to the ancient Greeks. The inheritance passed from Aristotle through his pupil, Theophrastus, and his successor, Crateuas, to Dioscorides (*fl.* AD 50–70), a Greek doctor. It was Dioscorides who made the first known list of medicinal herbs. Details of his life are somewhat obscure but it seems that he was a student at the University of Alexandria and later served in Nero's army. Since the medical school at Alexandria was founded as much on Egyptian medicine as on the current Greek teachings, Dioscorides' work contains learning of great antiquity.

His list of some five hundred plants contained in *De materia medica* was to remain the basis of herbal medicine for sixteen centuries. It is a work of the first importance in the history of Western medicine, and was the foundation stone upon which were based the English, French and German herbals, whose object was to help the reader to use easily obtained remedies to treat illness or injury. Nearly 2,000 years ago, Dioscorides was commending the strawberry for cleansing the blood and major bodily organs of impurities and for having a soothing effect on the temperament. The whole plant was imbued with spiritual properties. Until well into the seventeenth century, elucidating and commenting on the manuscript was the chief occupation of most of the herbalists in Europe.

The depositories of this herbal knowledge were the various religious communities. While the monks were busy studying and preserving ancient manuscripts, ordinary people were continuing to pass down their own herbal traditions. The earliest surviving Saxon medical work is the *Leechbook of Bald*, written in the tenth century. A 'leech' was a physician or someone who practised healing and this study is a mixture of charms, incantations and herbal remedies. Interestingly, many ills were thought to come flying through the air as 'elf shot'. The description is not unlike that of micro-organisms, whose discovery lay many centuries in the future. Among the herbs to be used when a charm was sung over a patient were strawberry leaves, which were considered to be effective also against goblins and nightmares.

Herbal of Apuleius Barbarius, c. 1100

The *colour* of the strawberry was thought to be very important; red was the colour of Thor and was abhorred by witches and all powers of darkness and evil. Using red wool or cloth to bind on healing herbs is an ancient custom. It was prescribed even as late as 1526 in the *Grete Herball*. The association of red with healing is still manifest today in the name and symbol of the Red Cross and in the blankets of most emergency ambulances.

Great powers were attributed also to the *odour* of various plants, including the wild strawberry. It was believed that plants' fragrances directly affected people's minds as well as curing the ills of their bodies.

Many of the old remedies were for flesh wounds; whether this was because life was rather dangerous in those days or because the tools of the average man's trade were crude, no one can say. One medical manuscript from before the fourteenth century gives a remedy using strawberries among thirty other ingredients ranging from henbane and groundsel to goatshoof.

The large-scale writing of new herbals began in Elizabethan times, when new plants – including the varieties of strawberry native to America – were being introduced and new concepts of the world and of the natural order of things were abounding.

In 1544 Pierandrea Mattioli (Matthiolus) wrote of the strawberry:

'It seemed good to me to receive this joyous and profitable plant into the bourgeoisie of my garden and to speak of it as follows: the leaves and the root cause to urinate and greatly serve the spleen; the decoction of the root, taken as a drink, helps inflammation of the liver and cleanses the kidneys and bladder; the juice of the strawberry cures blotches on the face.'

In his *Garden of Health*, published in London in 1579, William Langham prescribed the strawberry for a host of symptoms and ills. These included 'bladder griefs, to clean blood, help broken bones, shortness and stink of breathe, eyes, deformed face, hot fevers, gum griefs, mouth, sciatica, scabs, stomach ache, stone, sweating, teethache, thirst, throat, ill voices, urine stops, womens griefs, and wounds.' He considered that the best distillation of the berries was when they were ripe but not over-soft and that those found growing in the hilly woods were superior.

THE STRAWBERRY AND HEALTH

The herbal probably best known today is that of John Gerard, which appeared in 1597. In his *Herball* Gerard imbues the strawberry with these virtues:

'The leaves boiled and applied in manner of a poltice takes away the burning heat of wounds. A decoction of leaves strengthens the gums and helps hold the teeth.

The distilled water drunk with white wine is good against the passion of the heart, reviving the spirits, and making the heart merrie.

The ripe strawberries quench thirst, and take away, if often used, redness and heat of the face.

The leaves are good to put into lotions for mouth sores.'

Expressions such as 'to soothe the nerves' and 'to make the heart merrie' which are found in most herbals seem much more gentle and comforting terms than 'antidepressant' and 'to help increase libido'. Recent medical research can be interpreted as supporting ancient beliefs that there is a subtle interaction between suggestion, the body's chemistry and behavioural changes, so perhaps the very way in which we describe the effects of a remedy may play some part in the curative process. Science calls this the 'placebo effect' and some doctors claim that over 80 per cent of their treatments involve 'placebo medicine'; experts in psychosomatic medicine devote much time to its study. Our great-grandmothers would have found the jargon novel but not the effects it describes, for the connection between unhealthy states of mind and body was well accepted in their day.

John Parkinson, in his 1629 *Paradisi in sole Paradisus terrestris* (a punning

Gerard's 'Herball', 1597

title which translates as, roughly, 'park in the sun's earthly Paradise'), repeats some of Gerard's remedies but adds a few extra favourable remarks about the strawberry.

'The berries are excellent good to coole the liver, the bloud and spleene, or an hot chollericke stomacke to refresh and comfort the fainting spirits, and to quench thirst; they are good also for other inflammations, yet it behoveth one to be cauteous, or rather to refraine them in a feuer least by their putrefying in the stomacke, they encrease the fits and cause them to be the more fierce; the leaves and rootes boiled in wine and water and drunke doe likewise coole the liver and bloud and asswage all inflammation in the raines and bladder, provoketh urine, and allaieth the heate and sharpnesse thereof; the same also being drunke staieth the bloudy flixe and womens courses, and helpeth the swellings of the spleene; the water of the berries carefully distilled, is a soveraigne remedy and cordiall in the palpitations of the heart, that is, the panting and beating of the heart, and is good for the overflowing of the gall, the yellow jaundise.'

UNORTHODOX THEORISTS

During the sixteenth century 'Paracelsus' – a Swiss with the splendidly impressive name of Philippus Aureolus Theophrastus Bombastus von Hohenheim (1493–1541) – elaborated a traditional folk theory now generally known as the 'Doctrine of Signatures'. His version of it soon became a fashion throughout Europe. The general idea was that every plant was associated by colour, scent, habitat or shape with the disease it was 'designed' to cure. For example, strawberries were thought to effect

79

Eve in the garden from Parkinson's 'Paradisus Terrestris', 1629

the well-being of the blood on the grounds of their redness.

This doctrine confused our heritage of folk medicine and debased the work of previous herbalists because it gave plants curative properties which had not been tested down through the centuries. Mythology and eccentric theory became mixed up with empirical medicine.

But, like all theories, it found its disciples. Two of the most famous were William Coles and Nicholas Culpeper. Coles' work, published in 1657, was called *Adam in Eden*. In it he claims that strawberries are good for the overflowing of the gall which causes yellow jaundice and that the berries alone can cool down a feverish liver. He confirms many of Gerard's remedies but adds a cure for leprosy:

'The water of straw-berries distilled in a body of glass after they have stood in a bed of hot horsedung twelve or fourteen days cureth Lepry by Signaure [sic], if it be drunk, and the spots be bathed therewith.'

Culpeper declares in his 1653 herbal, originally called *A Physical Directory*, that the strawberry is so well known throughout the land that it needs no description, and that Venus owns the herb. At a stroke he both makes the plant common to everyman and imbues it with astrological significance. He says that the water of the berries, carefully distilled, is 'a sovereign remedy and cordial in the panting and beating of the heart, and is good for

🍓

yellow jaundice'. The berries themselves 'comfort the fainting spirits and quench thirst'. In other words, he echoes Parkinson. For mouth ulcers and sore throats he recommends a strawberry gargle; and he believes that solutions made from strawberry leaves and roots help fasten the teeth and strengthen the gums. For the eyes he gives a recipe for a lotion which, like the one which we have seen from Coles, needs immediate access to horses.

'Take so many strawberries as you shall think fitting and put them into a distillatory, or a body of glass fit for them, which being well closed, set it in a bed of horsedung for your use. It is an excellent water for inflamed eyes, and to take away a film or skin that beginneth to grow over them, and for such other defects in them, as may be helped by any outward medicine.'

Culpeper earned the acrimony of most of the orthodox medical men of his day. His first sin was to publish an unauthorized translation of the British College of Physicians' *Pharmacopoeia*. Secondly, he was an exponent of 'astrological botany', which ascribed to every plant a stellar or planetary influence. Teachings such as the Doctrine of Signatures and 'astrological botany' helped to bring herbal remedies into disfavour – particularly, much later, in Victorian times, when medical science was taking great strides and was eager to show contempt for the knowledge of earlier generations.

OF GREATER RESPECTABILITY

One physician whose works stayed long in favour was William Salmon, who published his herbal in two volumes in 1710 and 1711. He studied the recommendations of all the other herbalists and then listed what he felt were the most important virtues of the strawberry. These were:

The liquid juice for internal organs, including mouth ulcers.
A decoction of the roots, leaves and unripe fruit in water or wine as a general tonic.
The lotion of the juice for the gums and the washing of 'privities or other parts'.
Distilled water of the root for the eyes and face.
Ripe berries for the stomach and spleen.
A distillation of the berries for the skin.

'The Bath Scarlet'
by W. Hooker, 1817

Salmon suggests that a distillation of strawberries contains every virtue and so may be given two or three ounces (55–85g) at a time for most complaints.

In his *Useful Family Herbal* of 1754, John Hill repeats a great deal from earlier herbals but adds that an infusion of fresh strawberry leaves, taken in large quantities, flushes out the body through urine and is good in all cases of jaundice.

The British were not alone in making medical use of the strawberry.

In America, as we have seen, strawberries were among the most abundant of wild crops. A tea made from the whole plant was used by the Indians of western Washington to counter diarrhoea. Roger Williams, in his 1643 work on the languages of the Indians in New England, acclaimed their use of the strawberry. Early settlers in the New World, armed as they were with little more than herbals in the battle against illness, regarded medicinal herbs as extremely precious. Many plants were carefully imported from Britain and community leaders were often charged with the task of getting scarcer items. Even in the eighteenth century, national leaders such as Thomas Jefferson recorded appeals to them made by people searching for curative plants.

To glance briefly at the other side of the globe, the strawberry of the Far East, *Fragaria indica*, is used in China as an antiseptic and to counteract poisons from arrow-heads and snake-bites.

What's In a Strawberry?

Anything green that grew out of the mould
Was an excellent herb to our fathers of old.

Rudyard Kipling's often-quoted lines may well be true but is there any modern scientific basis for the use of the strawberry in medical treatment?

Laboratory analysis of the average strawberry shows that it contains almost 90 per cent water – more than milk does, for example. Next to water, the strawberry's chief constituents are acid salts, sugar and fibre. The breakdown is as follows:

water	89·500%
sugar	5·800%
cellulose and seeds	2·463%
soluble salts (including free acid)	1.146%
protein	0·800%
oily matter	0·154%
lime and iron salts	0·137%

(Obviously the exact percentages vary from strawberry to strawberry and, in a more general way, from species to species.)

The fruit sugar is more easily assimilated by people suffering from mild diabetes than is any other type of sugar. The salts are laxative, and with the seeds and fibre will stimulate sluggish bowels. The mineral salts present in the strawberry contain quite a high proportion of potassium, phosphoric acid and iron, so there is some scientific basis for the tradition that strawberries may have some tonic effect. The iron helps make the fruit red.

The strawberry contains a large amount of Vitamin C. Other vitamins present in the strawberry are Vitamin A, in the form of carotene (0·03mg per 100g), and Vitamin B_1 (thiamine; 0·01mg per 100g). Each 100g of fruit is equivalent to 26 Calories.

Strawberries are remarkably soluble in solutions similar to those of the alkaline digestive juices of the intestines; it can therefore be assumed with some confidence that they are good for digestion. However, unripe and unsound berries contain a much higher proportion of acid than does the perfect fruit and this probably accounts for the colic that some people get when they eat too many green or spoiled berries.

THE CURATIVE STRAWBERRY

During a stay in France recently I was told by two dinner guests about their painful attacks of gout. 'Help is at hand,' I said, setting before them bowls of fresh strawberries. They hardly believed that such an indulgence could do them good – but it did.

Being rich in salicylic acid, the strawberry has a favourable influence on the liver, the kidneys and the joints, and can therefore help many sufferers from gout, liver complaints, arthritis and rheumatism. The great Swedish botanist Linnaeus called them 'a blessing of the gods' after he was cured of gout by eating masses of strawberries morning and night.

Writing in 1931, Mrs M. Grieve in her *Modern Herball* (edited by Hilda Leyel, founder and for many years director of the Society of Herbalists) says that strawberries are invaluable in feverish conditions. In addition, she recommends the removal of discoloration of the teeth by affixing strawberries to them for about five minutes and then washing the mouth out with warm water to which has been added a pinch of bicarbonate of soda.

Mrs Grieve's editor, Hilda Leyel, writing in 1949 in her books for the Culpeper House herbal shops, groups the strawberry with the herbs known to alter the secretions of the thyroid, the adrenal glands, the spleen, and the salivary, submaxillary, prostate, parotid and other glands.

Here are some health uses of the strawberry.

IN CASES OF FEVER Mix the juices of strawberries and pomegranate leaves with some rosewater. Sip slowly.

KIDNEY AND GALL BLADDER STONES Stamp three or four good handfuls of the leaves in the bath, steep them in hot water and sponge the body from the hips upwards.

SHORTNESS OF BREATH Strawberry juice with white pepper will help this complaint.

A COLONIAL AMERICAN CURE FOR DIARRHOEA Modern medical botanists list the strawberry as effective against diarrhoea because the root is very astringent. The following nineteenth-century prescription – based on the use of the leaves – was used in the American Army.

Place ½lb (225g) of green wild strawberry leaves in two wine-glasses of good spirit. Boil this until it has reduced to a third. Strain and allow it to cool. Administer one tablespoonful every three hours until symptoms disappear. Usually about ten of these doses will be enough.

STRAWBERRY LEAF TEA Take a handful of fresh leaves from wild strawberry plants or cultivated alpines. Place in a two-cup teapot, pour in boiling water. Let brew for five minutes. Drink unsweetened to soothe and make mild your disposition.

It is a waste of time using tap water to prepare herbal brews, because the chemicals used to recycle domestic water destroy many natural plant properties. Use a still spring water instead. There are numerous good bottled ones on the market.

When rewarming any herbal brew, never boil it. Pouring boiling water over herbs is *not* the same as boiling them, which is akin to stewing and does nothing but remove healing properties.

STRAWBERRY ROOT AND LEAF INFUSION Use wild strawberry plants, if you can get them, or second-year garden ones, provided they have been grown without the use of insecticides or chemical fertilizers. Wash the roots and put them with a handful of leaves into a non-metal bowl. Cover with 1¾ pints (1 litre) of boiling water and let brew for about eight minutes.

Drinking a small cupful will help purify the blood and stimulate the gut. The infusion may give a reddish tint to the urine.

STRAWBERRY TOOTHPASTE

Teeth can benefit from regular brushing with strawberries. First, to strengthen the gums, mix a handful of dried, powdered leaves and roots of the wild berry, sprinkle your toothbrush with this and brush your teeth and gums well. It will not damage the enamel nor turn your teeth red. If this is too much trouble, then simply chew a few berries and let them stay in your mouth for a few minutes. Your lips and mouth will feel fresh and the treatment benefits the gums. Support for this remedy – and for the claims of all the old herbal writers concerning the effects of strawberries on the teeth and gums – comes from modern orthodox dentistry. One American medical study – *Medical Botany* (1977) – says that the roots and leaves, used as lotions and gargles, help fasten loose teeth.

THE CURATIVE STRAWBERRY IN RUSSIA

Russian folk medicine uses the fruit, roots and leaves of the strawberry to treat a wide variety of complaints. In both the Soviet Union and Bulgaria, the study of the strawberry in medicine is considered a serious matter and research into its use has been encouraged. Here are its most important uses.

LIVER Diet is of first importance in the treatment of liver complaints and strawberries are particularly good if taken as a drink on a regular daily basis. Make a decoction of stems and leaves in boiling water, allowing it to steep for fifteen minutes. Drink up to two or three cups a day, while the liquid is hot.

DROPSY This is a complaint which results from water-retention, so any food which helps cause sweating should be freely taken. The fruit of the strawberry is especially good for this.

GOUT Gout is characterized by increased levels of uric acid in the bloodstream and, unsurprisingly, anything that increases these levels such as excessive meat consumption should be avoided. Strawberries and gooseberries, when in season, should be generously consumed.

COUGH One of the very oldest Siberian remedies uses several different kinds of berries in the treatment of coughs. First combine bilberry or cranberry juice in equal parts with clear honey and take one tablespoonful of this mixture three or four times daily. Throughout this treatment you should drink as much wild-strawberry-leaf tea as you want. Sweeten the tea, if you must, with a little honey, but bear in mind that it is only in this century that our palates have been spoiled by the oversweetening of so many foods.

REMEDIES FOR CHILDREN

Strawberries can help in many complaints of the young.

TO PREVENT CHILBLAINS During the summer, rub the part of the body usually affected with crushed strawberries and apply strawberry poultices overnight. The child will smell delicious and when winter comes there will be far fewer complaints about chilblains.

A GOOD PRIEST'S HEALTH DRINK FOR CHILDREN 'Pick a generous

*'The Strawberry Girl' by
Sir Joshua Reynolds, 1773*

handful of wild strawberry leaves, or use dried ones. Pour ½ pint [300ml; about 1cup] of boiling water over them and leave for fifteen minutes. Strain, and then stir into this pure strawberry liquid some hot milk and a very little honey'. A good health drink liked by children of all ages. If they are allergic to cow's milk – and many children are – then use goat's milk. It will almost certainly not upset them.

NOSEBLEEDS AND BEDWETTING
An old country tradition has it that nosebleeding can be stopped by holding a strawberry root about an inch long in the mouth. Children who wet the bed should be given an infusion of leaves as a tea once a day for three days.

Even in the 1980s, the use of the strawberry as medicine continues to be held in high esteem with two modern French herbalists, Maurice Messegue and Jean Palaiseul, both commending its beneficial properties. Messegue says that the fruit is nutritious, cooling and soothing, and recommends its use in a poultice for ulcers and wounds. Palaiseul writes that strawberries, with their high iron content, can be recommended for people suffering from anaemia, and says that 10½–18oz (300–500g; 1¾–2 cups) of the fresh fruit eaten daily for a month is excellent for chronic gastroenteritis.

When we use the strawberry to benefit our health and beauty we follow the custom of centuries. Professor Agnes Arber of Cambridge University, in her study *Herbals, Their Origin and Evolution* (1912), remarked that the herbal traditions of the ancient Greeks have come down to us almost unaltered over 2,000 years. Yet we may still claim, as the Roman writer Seneca did, that 'the day will yet come when our descendants will be amazed that we remained ignorant of things that will to them seem so plain'.

No doubt the uses of the strawberry will still be among those things.

DANGEROUS STRAWBERRIES

ALLERGIES

Many people get urticaria (nettle rash or hives), a disorder of the skin resembling the eruptions caused by a nettle's sting, through eating strawberries. This symptom can be accompanied by itching and irritation.

Most frequently the face and neck are affected by the rash, which can last for a few hours or several days. Until further research has been done, the easiest solution for people who break out in a rash after eating strawberries is to stop eating them. If you suffer a reaction, allay the local irritation by sponging with calamine lotion or with a teaspoonful of soda to a glass of warm water, or by rubbing with menthol.

The strawberry turns up as a part of the names of several medical conditions. The strawberry mark we have met. Other examples are 'strawberry gall bladder', which refers to deposits of cholesterol in the gall bladder; and 'strawberry tongue', the characteristic appearance of the tongue in scarlet fever, where its tip and edges turn bright red and the rest of it is coated.

There is another condition where the strawberry is a little more directly involved – 'strawberry picker's foot drop'. This is a relatively common disorder in the English fens and in Finland during strawberry harvesting: it involves a weakness and tingling in the feet following prolonged periods of strawberry picking. It results in a nerve palsy due to pressure from squatting for long periods, and can turn into a serious neurological disorder.

If you enjoy gathering 'pick-your-own' farm berries, do think about strawberry picker's foot drop, because the damage to the legs can be permanent. You should stop picking the moment any tingling or other sensation occurs anywhere in your feet or legs.

GATHERING, DRYING AND STORING THE STRAWBERRY PLANT

In ancient times the strawberry was gathered from the wild by herb-gatherers and drug-sellers. Many of the superstitions which have been handed down to us about gathering wild plants probably stem from the desire of these workers to protect their trade.

Nevertheless, if you want to use herbs for medicinal purposes, it is no use going about their gathering and storage in just any way that fancy takes you. There are many time-tested methods which ensure that the herbs' healing properties remain potent.

Wild strawberries are more powerful than cultivated ones. Gather them on a dry, hot day, away from orchards and other cultivated areas where chemical fertilizers and insecticides may have been used, perhaps over a long period. Don't tread on any wild flowers as you search and remember that it is a criminal offence for anyone in Britain to uproot wild plants without the express permission of the owner or occupier of the land on which they grow. The wild strawberry is not a protected species, but you should still respect its conservation.

Gently lift the whole plant, taking care not to bruise the leaves or let the fruit drop away. Place the plants in a wicker or reed basket – *not* a plastic bag, which may contain contaminating chemicals and will start to 'sweat' from the natural heat generated by the plants.

When you get home, spread the plants quickly in a single layer in the shade. Do not wash them and keep them well away from each other. Turn them over the first few days. The roots should be cut up after they have dried a little in direct sunshine. If they are allowed to dry completely, they will be too tough to cut. Store when all are perfectly dry, otherwise mildew will ruin the lot.

STRAWBERRIES FOR BEAUTY

For thousands of years women have used strawberries to care for their bodies and enhance the quality of their skins. This is not surprising for the pH (acidity) of the strawberry is almost exactly the same as that of the skin itself.

Beauty recipes from earliest times speak of crushing the berries together with oatmeal or in combination with other things to produce an array of improving effects. In Victorian England, the strawberry was considered second only to that of human milk as a freckle-remover. With their high and favourable acidity and Vitamin C content, strawberries are ideal for bleaching, softening and nourishing the skin.

STRAWBERRY CONDITIONING CREAM

Melt 1 dessertspoonful (10ml) of lanolin in a double boiler. Add the same quantity of oatmeal and, when the mixture is smooth, stir in ½ cup (120ml; 4fl oz) fresh strawberry juice, beating all the time. When cool, apply to the face and the back of the hands. Leave for two hours and then wash away with tepid water or, better yet, fresh rosewater.

SUNBURN CARE

For mild sunburn, take a few fresh strawberries and rub them over the affected areas. Leave the juice on for at least half an hour. Wash it off with warm water.

STRAWBERRY CREAM FOR OILY OR NORMAL SKIN

Take a handful of fresh strawberries and wipe them over to remove any loose dirt. Mash them up and strain the juice out through a muslin bag. Heat ½oz (15g) white beeswax, 1½oz (40g) sweet almond oil and 1oz (30g) apricot kernel oil together in a double boiler until the wax is melted. Remove from the heat and very quickly add the strawberry juice. Beat this mixture until it turns creamy and fluffy. Add 8 drops of tincture of benzoin; then continue beating until the mixture is cool, or else it will curdle and you will have to start all over again.

Store the cream in glass or pottery jars, not metal or plastic containers. It will keep for upwards of three months.

STRAWBERRY MILK LOTION

With the introduction of distillation, skin lotions and tonics became very popular. From the Middle Ages until the nineteenth century, most women distilled or dispensed them, and every house had a still-room where such things were made. Waters for the complexion were distilled from a wide variety of things, including rosemary, bean-flowers, vine leaves, lilies, borage, tansy, eggs, goat's milk – and strawberries.

Hilda Leyel, in her *The Magic of Herbs* (1926), said that to preserve the complexion you should bathe your face with strawberry juice. Leave it on overnight and wash in the morning with chervil water.

To make an excellent strawberry milk lotion, extract the juice from some fresh berries and add a little warmed milk. Apply to your face and let it stay on overnight – or at least for a few hours – and then rinse it off with rosewater.

STRAWBERRY FACE MASK

In his herbal of 1579 William Langham notes that strawberries have long been commended for beautifying the skin. He says that face pimples may be treated by putting the ripe strawberries into a 'leape of green rushes and hanging it against a wall where the sun has most power over a glass', and then anointing the face with the resulting water.

The secret of the strawberry face mask described here is to allow it to work as you sleep.

Mash a cup of fresh ripe berries in an equal amount of spring water. Pat on the face before you retire. The dried mixture can be washed away the next morning. It is also effective for softening skin which has been exposed to too much sun. According to legend, an application of the mixture to your shoulders and bosom will make you 'as fair as a young maiden'.

VENUS OBSERVED

Perhaps Mme Tallier, one of Marie Antoinette's ladies-in-waiting, knew that the strawberry belonged to Venus, for she is said to have bathed in the juice of strawberries and raspberries. Afterwards she was gently washed with sponges soaked in milk and perfumes, her skin glowing sensually pink from the fruit. If this seems too extravagant to try, then here is an old recipe for a face wash which may have a similar effect.

Take about 14oz (425g; 3½ cups) of wild strawberries, a handful of tansy and 3 pints (1.75 litres; 3¾ pints) of goat's milk and distil together over a low flame. Bathe your face in the liquid each morning, ending with a gentle wash of warm water.

The ultimate strawberry from Bosch's 'Garden of Earthly Delights'

Top: William Morris fabric, 'The Strawberry Thief', 1883.
Above left: detail from a sampler, English, 17th century.
Above right: Strawberries placed in a curious conjunction with the
mythical cockatrice (detail of Valence, 1631–1640)

FOUR

ART AND THE STRAWBERRY

If you can draw a strawberry
you can draw anything
John Ruskin (1819–1900)

In art the strawberry has no season. From ancient Roman pots to modern advertisements it remains a favourite with artists and craftsmen of every kind. You might have difficulty deciding if someone had drawn a blackberry or a raspberry but not a strawberry. The heart-shaped fruit is instantly recognisable when drawn by the least talented. It seems to have been the easiest of objects to portray whether in early medical herbals or in embroidered samplers executed by little girls in the eighteenth century.

The colour of the strawberry is famous. Painters and craftsmen have no monopoly here. There are strawberry roan horses, a strawberry face referring to someone suffering from dyspepsia or high blood pressure, the strawberry pear, the bass, the cockle, the crab and the finch – to name but a few.

Why an artist chooses to show a strawberry usually dictates how he portrays it. It may be realistically as in a botanical study, symbolically for religious purposes or merely as a decorative motif. In the ancient world when the strawberry was recorded for its medicinal benefits, the leaf, fruit and roots are all shown in a highly stylized and plain manner – presumably so the reader could be easily guided to the plant in the wild. This way of showing the strawberry continued in illustrated herbals and in embroideries until well after naturalism in art became popular.

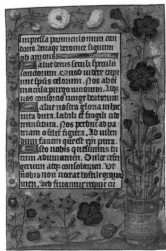

'Manderscheid Hours', c. 1500, previously in the collection of Prince Fürstenberg

MEDIAEVAL STRAWBERRIES

'Naturalism' began to appear first in the religious works of mediaeval art in the borders of prayer books and the foreground of religious paintings. A fine example is *The Adoration of the Lamb*, the Ghent Altarpiece of 1426–1432 by Hubert and Jan van Eyck. These artist brothers brought people a new grasp of the visible world in their paintings: the wild strawberries in the altarpiece are perfectly portrayed among the flowers and fruit of the mediaeval garden, which is shown as the field of paradise. Such plants must have been drawn directly from nature for they are exact and fresh.

The strawberry was widely favoured by many book illumination artists during the Middle Ages. Here are just a few of the outstanding examples still extant which feature the plant: borders of berries in *Le Grand Coutumier de Normandie*, illuminated in Rouen, 1460–1470; *The Castelnau Breviary* written at Troyes in about 1480 for Jouvenal des Ursins; *Legnage Heurs* painted in Central France about 1420; and the *Heures de Jacques de Bregilles*, probably done in Brussels in 1442.

Among the works of the French master, Jean Bourdichon, or that of his followers featuring strawberries are *Les Grandes Heures de la Reine* of Anne of Brittany (1508), *Vierge à l'Enfant-Encadrement de Fraises*, showing the Virgin Mary opposite a page of text bordered with strawberries, and *The Great Book of Hours* of Henry VIII of England. In another work, the *Hours of Tours* (Paris 1514), the Holy Family is depicted with Mary holding up what appears to be a strawberry as the symbol of her love and purity.

The strawberry fruit and leaf was especially favoured for a variety of embroidered and painted household and personal items. These included clothing, chests, boxes, book covers and fruit trenchers.

Fruit trenchers were small wooden plates used by the Elizabethans at the conclusion of a special feast for 'fruit and conceits of all sorts'. The decorations are elaborately painted with a biblical reference in the centre to enlighten the gathering or witty passages called 'poesies' to amuse everyone.

At the end of the meal each guest read aloud the 'poesy' on his trencher. One set in the collection of the Bodleian Library at the Ashmolean Museum, Oxford, is decorated with splendid gold strawberries symmetrically arranged in each corner. Part of the inscription reads:

Deal not wrongly with they neighbor
with meteyard, weight, or measure
Levit. 19:35

God knoweth both the deceiver and
him that is deceived.
Job 12:16

Elizabethan trenchers, c. 1600

95

BOTANICAL STUDIES

In spite of the use of the strawberry in so many domestic ways, paintings of fruit were not widely popular until the end of the sixteenth century when the Dutch and Flemish schools of still life painting began. The keen interest in flower gardens between 1750 and 1850 also helped create demand. With so many painters, further specialization occurred and some devoted their skills to certain aspects of flowers or fruit. For example, Carlos von Riefel, an Austrian, excelled in foliage. His painting of the strawberry, *F. grandiflora*, is an outstanding example. Such is his realism that the minute defects in leaves from insect bites are clearly visible.

Hunting for the strawberry in art can be compulsive. During a moderately unpleasant examination by my doctor, he interpreted my gasp as related to his professional intrusion when it was simply the result of my discovering – while in a prone position – that the strawberry was the motif in his plasterwork ceiling.

NEEDLEWORK STRAWBERRIES

As accomplished as all the paintings and botanical drawings of the strawberry may be, the plant really comes into its own in applied and

Left: 'A Dragon Fly and Other Insects with Wild Strawberries'
by Jan van Kessel (1626–1679)
Above: 'Fragaria Grandiflora' by Carlos von Riefel, 1903

Above: English sampler, mid-18th century.
Opposite above: Wedgwood have used strawberry motifs in different
patterns since 1806. Below: Carl Fabergé's 'Vase of Strawberries',
sold in 1977 for £36,000

decorative art, especially household and personal objects. Most often, this is in the work of the gifted amateur and pre-eminent among the techniques used are those of the needle and loom.

Even when colour is not used – such as in 'broderie anglaise' which consists of open-work spaces in various shapes and sizes – the strawberry is relatively easy to spot. In Ayrshire whitework a variety of strawberries was often symmetrically arranged and the outline of the fruit or leaf filled in with various needle-made surface textures. This type of embroidery, fashionable from the eighteenth century until about the time of the American Civil War, and still so today in Sweden and Denmark, was worked in white cotton thread on a white cotton ground. The effect is like intricate lace. Whitework was done on articles of clothing and innumerable household objects. The designs were generally drawn from nature and certain plants, particularly oak leaves, acorns and strawberries, are almost traditional. Such needlework greatly damaged eyesight and James Morris in *The Art of Ayrshire White Needlework* (1916) tells how workers 'bathe their eyes with whisky, notwithstanding the sharpness of the pain, because of the relief afforded and the temporary quickening of the sight'.

Using the strawberry for decoration was not just the province of stitching gentle-women and trained artisans. Children, too, found the berry a familiar inspiration. Marjorie Reeves, in her book *Sheep Bell and Ploughshire*, describes how one Master Thomas Whitaker, aged 13, practised his copperplate during September 1790 by making out invoices for goods to imaginary characters such as 'Madam Strawberry bought of Manywords Milliner'. His sister, Anna, completed an embroidered sampler of the Lord's Prayer that same year, framing the words with a delicate border of strawberries.

Strawberry plates, bowls, spoons and dishes against a late 19th-century embroidered cloth from Kashmir

Shape, size, colour, form and religious attributes all combined to make the strawberry fruit, leaf and flower a great favourite with sampler embroiderers from the sixteenth century to the twentieth century. The reason for this long artistic tradition of associating the strawberry plant in part or in whole with the Holy Family is well described by Elizabeth Haig in her *Floral Symbolism of the Great Masters* (1916): a 'very perfect fruit with neither thorns nor stone, but sweet, soft and delicious all through and through. Its flowers are of the whiteness of innocence and its leaves almost of the sacred trefoil form and since it grows upon the ground, there is no possibility of its being the dread fruit of the Tree of Knowledge. Its meaning always appears to be that of perfect righteousness.'

Transient pleasure though it may be, the eating rather than the painting of strawberries is after all our ultimate and most satisfactory relationship with this sweet fruit. The remark of one American southerner, Josh Billings, as reported in 1917 expresses the conviction of most people:

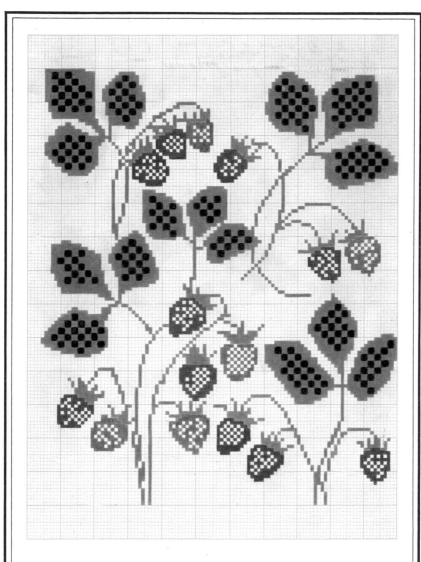

This embroidery design can be worked in wool or silk to the canvas stitch size desired. It makes a useful cushion or, in repeat using embroidery cotton on linen, a pretty tablecloth

'. . . the man who kan eat strawberry, besprinkled with Kream (at someboddy's else expense) and not lay his hand on his stummuck and thank the Author of strawberries and stummucks, iz a man with a worn-out conscience – a man whose mouth tastes like a hole in the ground, and don't care what gose down it.'

Strawberries in America have had a large number of inappropriate and freak names. 'In 1882, T. T. Lyon indignantly branded the name of a recently introduced sort, *Big Bob*, as "rowdyish and an outrage upon propriety". Nothing daunted, the originator of this euphorious variety proceeded to inflict upon the public a seedling of it, which he named *Big Bob's Baby*.'

Top: A panel from an American 19th century Bride's Quilt.
Above: Strawberries galore. English handkerchief; American pencil;
plastic buttons; thimbles; enamelled boxes and clockcase; Victorian
pincushions; needle-sharpener; greetings card; and a European
Silk Commission invitation

FIVE

THE STRAWBERRY IN THE GARDEN

> . . . there be divers sorts of strawberries; one red,
> another white, a third sort greene, and likewise a wilde
> strawberry which is altogether barren of fruit.
>
> *John Gerard, 'Herball', 1597*

Wild strawberries may have an incomparable fragrance and sweetness, but the gardener, if he or she wants abundant crops, standardization of size and flavour and a long harvesting season, must turn to those varieties in whose history mankind has played a part.

In 1925, just over two hundred years since Frézier had landed in Marseille with his carefully nurtured Chilean plants, there were 1,362 cultivated varieties of strawberries to choose from in America. Since then, the list has grown on both sides of the Atlantic with many old varieties being dropped and better new ones added every year.

Over the centuries, odd varieties have been developed whose value is more of curiosity than anything else. The 'Plymouth' strawberry produces minute leaflets and red fruit. It was first spotted in a garden in Plymouth, England, and was recorded in the 1633 edition of Gerard's *Herball*. Elsewhere, seedlings have been raised with five leaflets as Charles Darwin noted in his *Variation of Animals and Plants under Domestication* (1868). There is a double-flowered variety, *Fragaria coucou*, a sterile variety, and one with white fruit.

Man has long liked 'mammoth' berries. In 1613 a strawberry of diameter $1\frac{3}{8}$ inches (3.5cm) was duly reported in the *Hortus Eystettensis*. In

Left: 'Treatise on Berry Culture', T. Haynes, 1823.
Right: The Chile strawberry from Frézier's Journal published in 1722

Quadripartitum Botanicum (1708) Simon Pallus, a Dane, claimed to have seen strawberries 'which produced a fruit nearly the size of the peach'.

Since Victorian days, the main aim of strawberry breeders has been to obtain fruit of uniform size together with simultaneous maturation of the crop – both of which are vital aspects for commercial growers. In recent times, with mechanization of picking, the development of new varieties has been done chiefly at government-sponsored research stations. In his University of California study, *Plants, Man and Life* (1954), Edgar Anderson has no hesitation in declaring that the new strains of strawberry are 'the one crop of world importance to have originated in modern time'.

THE STRAWBERRY ITSELF

The strawberry plant is divided into roots, stolon (runner), leaves, flowers and fruit.

In many cultivated varieties the flowers lack stamens and the fruits do not develop unless pollinated from another variety. Many varieties are distinguished by some aspect of the plant as a whole. For example it may be tall or dwarf, or compact or spreading in habit. The ideal variety should be vigorous, hardy, productive, immune to diseases in the region where it is grown, and pleasing in taste, texture and aroma.

The runners gradually extend around the mother plant, and from them develop the shoots and roots. The runner is a part of the parent until it decays – by which time it has built a large colony, as the new contractile roots pull the young plants firmly down into the soil. This method of propagation does not allow individual plants to distribute their progeny widely; but in most parts of the world the strawberry has managed to survive by this process.

There are no true climbing strawberries, only varieties with extremely long runners which can be tied up to produce a 'climbing' effect.

Varieties to Choose

There are now so many good strawberry varieties that the amateur gardener can be overwhelmed. The list changes from year to year, depending on the demand for particular varieties and the advent of new ones onto the market. Some are available in one country but not another.

New varieties take time to gain favour and the list of available ones is constantly changing. Of the twelve varieties most widely recommended by gardening writers in 1939 only one, 'Royal Sovereign', is still available. Fashion plays its part, too: the alpines and perpetual varieties are now beginning to find favour in Britain, thanks in large part to the greater notice given to them by food and gardening writers and to the appearance of these smaller fruits in trend-setting restaurants.

It is in the interest of all amateur gardeners to keep up sufficient demand for a wide range of strawberry varieties. In this way commercial suppliers will continue to make available many delicious and *different* ones. Availability of varieties is based on realistic demand and not necessarily on the supplier's own vision of the ideal strawberry (although the suppliers, like all strawberry enthusiasts, each have their favourites).

Varieties suitable for growing in Britain are not usually right for America and *vice versa*, although those from America's eastern seaboard may do well in Britain.

Strawberry varieties can be divided into three groups: the common garden strawberries, such as the 'Cambridge' varieties, that fruit in June and July; the alpines, such as 'Baron Solemacher', which fruit from June until November; and the *remontants*, or perpetual strawberries, which fruit from May until November. These latter – which are *not* alpines – are called 'ever-bearers' in America and sometimes 'autumn-bearers' in Britain.

COMMON GARDEN STRAWBERRIES

'Cambridge Rival' and 'Cambridge Late Pine' will likely remind you of the taste of *fraises de bois*.

'CAMBRIDGE FAVOURITE' This is the standard against which new varieties are usually judged. Mid-season. Rounded, large, evenly shaped pink-red fruits. Fair flavour and sweet when fully ripe. A reliable and heavy-cropping variety. June/July fruiting. Good for barrels and container-growing. Excellent for jam and suitable for preserving and freezing.

'CAMBRIDGE LATE PINE' Strong grower, good crop, fruit round and red. Resistant to frost and mildew. Late June/July fruiting.

'CAMBRIDGE RIVAL' Early. Large crimson fruits which slowly ripen to dark red. Good flavour. Very suitable for growing under cloches or for forcing. June/July fruiting.

'CAMBRIDGE VIGOUR' Large, glossy scarlet fruits with red flesh and a slightly acid flavour. Suitable for growing under cloches. An early ripener in the first season with a smaller crop in subsequent years. June/July fruiting.

'DIASTRAR' An early good cropper with medium-large berries of excellent flavour.

'DOMANIL' A heavy cropper from Belgium. Large, firm fruit with a moderate flavour. Not particularly good for freezing. Late mid-season.

'GORELLA' Strong grower. Mid-season. Large fruit, bearing an even crop during the season.

'GRANDEE' One of the largest-fruiting varieties in common cultivation. Scarlet-crimson fruit with a good flavour and less acid than 'Royal Sovereign'. In its second year it makes too much growth to be grown under cloches, but on a good loamy soil it may yield 3lb (1.35kg) per plant. A good one for local horticultural shows. Fruits early in June/July.

'HAPIL' A Belgian variety. Large berries with a fine flavour. High yield. Mid-season. Liked by commercial growers.

'A Basket of French Strawberries' by Victoria Whiteaker, 1982

'LITESSA' A West German berry, fruiting mid-season. A very heavy cropper. Good flavour.

'PANTAGRUELLA' A West German introduction. A compact grower with medium-size fruit of excellent flavour. The earliest cropper. The plants are compact so set them closer together than normal – about 9 inches (23cm) apart.

'REDGAUNTLET' Early mid-season. A heavy cropper. Large, scarlet-crimson fruits with white flesh. Bred in Scotland and especially suitable for northerly conditions. June/July fruiting. Some resistance to disease. May produce an autumn crop if cloches have been used in the spring or if the summer has been very hot.

'ROYAL SOVEREIGN' Early mid-season. Superb large, wedge-shaped scarlet fruits. Still a favourite with amateur gardeners on account of its flavour. It is often a comparatively poor cropper. When forced, it can be difficult but usually gives a good crop. Many leading suppliers have given up stocking 'Royal Sovereign' because it is susceptible to virus diseases and botrytis.

'TALISMAN' Late mid-season. This vigorous grower may be the answer for the forgetful gardener. It seems to survive well among weeds yet does

not like being planted in matted rows. Medium-sized, conical deep-scarlet fruits with an excellent flavour, although the fruit is inclined to be soft. June/July fruiting. Resistant to red-core disease.

'TAMELLA' A strong-growing Dutch berry, good for forcing and growing in cloches. The fruit is firm and wedge-shaped, red to orange, and has good flavour. High yield. An all-purpose berry for dessert, freezing, bottling and jam. June/July fruiting.

'TENIRA' Another Dutch variety. Late mid-season fruiting. A heavy cropper with crimson berries of good flavour. Disease-resistant.

ALPINES

Alpines are the easiest of all strawberries to grow and for sheer flavour are hard to beat. They thrive in the shade and damp-soil, and live happily in borders, pots, tubs or window-boxes. A bed of their own is a rare treat.

They crop remarkably well over a four-month season. Unlike other strawberries, most alpine varieties do not increase themselves by runners, but you can divide existing plants in the spring. Plants raised from seed will produce fruit for four years.

The choice in Britain is usually limited to 'Baron Solemacher', but occasionally other varieties can be found. Try 'Alexandria', 'Pineapple Crush', or 'Yellow Wonder'. I personally like 'Alexandria', which is tall and a strong grower, and has large, sweet berries. Some plants of this variety have cropped well for me over a period of three or four years. You can obtain other alpine varieties from French seed suppliers.

'BARON SOLEMACHER' A vigorous, runnerless alpine variety. The very small, bright-crimson aromatic fruits are held off the ground. A heavy cropper. Late July/October fruiting. Grows best in shade. There is always room in a cottage garden for more plants so I stick in 'Baron Solemacher' here and there.

PERPETUALS

While the English concentrated on developing the summer-fruiting strawberries, the French devoted their attention to perpetual-fruiting varieties, or *fraisiers à gros fruits remontants*. These are large-fruited autumn-bearing varieties.

French growers based the development of their *remontants* on the alpine strawberry, but the early part of the story is obscure. It is said that one

19th-century strawberry punnets

Abbé Thivolet, a parish priest of Chenôves in Saône-et-Loire, in 1893 produced a prolonged-flowering variety by crossing an alpine with an English variety. Such cross-fertilization between the two types would have resulted in sterile seed, so it seems likely that the Abbé's variety was the product of an accidental but fortunate cross-fertilization in which he played no conscious part.

Whatever the case, the Abbé's variety – 'St Joseph' – was the first perpetual large-fruited strawberry and is still a berry worthy of cultivation. From this variety developed many others, including 'St Antoine-de-Padoue', a cross between 'St Joseph' and 'Royal Sovereign'. Remarkable modern achievements include 'Suavis', 'Merveille de France', 'Pacifique' and 'Record'. A single 'Record' plant can take up a square yard (0.8sq m) and an acre can bear twenty tons of berries (about 50 tonnes a hectare).

In America the perpetuals have their own history. At the turn of the century, Samuel Cooper of western New York State developed 'Pan-American'. Eventually, America produced the large and vigorous 'Red Rich'. Austria and Germany, too, have produced new perpetuals since the 1920s, and one, 'Kuntner's Triumph', has been commercially valuable.

Perpetuals' horticultural requirements are similar to those of summer-fruiting varieties, but they are heavy feeders and intolerant of draughts. The Royal Horticultural Society suggests 'Gento', 'La Sans Rivale', 'St Claude' and 'Rabunda' as a good selection for planting. Plant in the spring and remove any blossoms found before the end of May in the first year; the first crop should be ready in August. Do not remove leaves in late August, as with summer-fruiting varieties: do this instead in late winter. Cloching in September will add two or three weeks to the picking season.

There are many varieties of perpetuals. Here are notes on just a few. 'AROMEL' Autumn-fruiting perpetual, bred by Richard Cumberland of Dorset. A good cropper with medium-sized fruit of outstanding flavour. 'GENTO' An autumn-fruiting variety. Large, red, medium-firm fruits

with a slightly acid flavour; can yield up to 3lb (1.35kg) per plant. Berries are also carried on the runners while these remain attached to the parent plants. July/October fruiting. Watch for mildew. Will grow in lime soil.
'HAMPSHIRE MAID' Small to medium-sized, sweet crimson fruit. Crops best when the autumn is warm. Not suitable for heavy soils. Requires lots of water.
'LA SANS RIVALE' A moderately strong-growing perpetual with very small leaves; crops heavily. The long, conical bright-red berries are small, with pink flesh and good flavour. Eat fruit the same day as picked. July/October fruiting, but if then protected by cloches often continues into November. Best planted every year. Irrigate well during dry months.

NEW VARIETIES

Varieties come and go. Some are lost forever, but there are new ones to take their places. The Dutch have developed 'Maxim' which has large, firm, juicy fruit of excellent colour. It has been called 'the strawberry of the 1980s'. Ken Muir, a leading British grower, expects another Dutch variety, 'Rapella', to prove the superior autumn-fruiting variety of the future. Yet another Dutch variety, 'Bogata', which has large late-season fruits, is expected to help extend the season.

Thanks to a breeding programme seeking to develop resistance to red-core and other diseases, the Scottish Horticultural Research Institute has developed four new varieties, 'Saladin', 'Silver Jubilee', 'Tantallon' and 'Troubadour'.

CERTIFIED STOCK

Whatever variety you choose in the end, it is important to purchase plants from a reliable supplier who can be trusted to provide virus-free, healthy stock. Certain varieties of strawberry carry a certificate of health and are thus called 'certified stock'. The certification scheme is run in Britain by the Ministry of Agriculture, Fisheries and Food. It raises virus-free plants and distributes root-stock to growers for propagation. The growers raise the new young stock, for which they get the health certificate, and the plants are then sold to the public.

This scheme is very important for the commercial grower and fruit farmer, less so for the amateur. However, where possible buy varieties on the certification list which, you should note, changes frequently. If the

'Fragaria virginiana' from Laxtons' 'The Strawberry Manual'

varieties you want are not on the list, plant what you like and take a gamble.

There is not a certificate plan for perpetuals, so the Royal Horticultural Society advises that it is best to assume that they are carrying virus. You should therefore plant them away from beds of summer-fruiting certified stock.

A MATTER OF TASTE

Most gourmets agree that wild strawberries – from wood or from mountain – are the first choice for taste, with the alpines a close second. After that, each cultivar has its own devotees.

In 1982 a group of amateur and professional fruit enthusiasts gathered at the Royal Horticultural Society's garden in Wisley, England, to make an unofficial assessment of a number of modern varieties. The tasters were not told until afterwards the names of the different strawberries. A large number of people were involved so their opinion is significant. Here, in descending order of preference, is the list: 'Hapil'; 'Royal Sovereign'; 'Cambridge Vigour'; 'Tenira'; 'Tamella'; 'Cambridge Favourite'; 'Aromel'; 'Redgauntlet'; 'Marmion'; 'Templar'; 'Tantallon'; 'Talisman'; 'Domanil'; 'Saladin'; 'Litessa'; 'Harvester'.

A straw bedding helps keep the fruit clean

In unofficial tasting sessions held in 1977 and 1980, 'Royal Sovereign' came first, 'Cambridge Rival' and 'Aromel' in joint second place, and 'Cambridge Late Pine' third.

In America, Maryland, Michigan and California are leading centres of commercial strawberry growing. You should contact your local county or state Agricultural Extension Service for the varieties most suitable for your area. American varieties of merit include 'Earliglow', 'Redchief', 'Guardian', 'Midway', 'Allstar', 'Surecrop', 'Tennessee Beauty', 'Shasta', 'Tioga' and 'Northwest'. It is strongly recommended that any variety you purchase be resistant to or tolerant of two soil-borne fungus diseases: red stele and verticillium.

COMMERCIAL GROWING

With the increasing use of home freezers and the ever-expanding market for commercial frozen foods, strawberry development in recent years has focused on varieties which offer exceptional freezing qualities. The 'Totem' is one such new cultivar. It was developed at Canada's Department of Agriculture research station in British Columbia and is an unusually dark berry. Another cultivar from the same area is 'Shuksan'.

The major concerns of commercial strawberry growers remain consistent quality, heavy cropping and the improvement of plants which are suitable for mechanical harvesting and processing. Research on new varieties is continuous in America and Europe. The increasing expense of commercial harvesting coupled with the general public's enthusiasm for 'pick-your-own' crops in Britain has led to more commercial holdings outside the traditional areas of Kent, Norfolk, Hereford, Cambridgeshire, Essex and Lincolnshire. The estimated output in 1978 from a total of 14,000 acres was worth nearly £34 million.

British market prices in April are now affected each year by imports of strawberries from America, Southern Europe and the Middle East. Many specialist farmers therefore send their first high-value fruit to market and then let the public in to pick the second crop.

THE STRAWBERRY BED

Like all plants, the strawberry is greatly influenced by every element in its growing environment. The same variety can, even under apparently similar conditions, produce wide variations in fruit yield.

POSITION OF THE BED

Strawberries grow low where the air is coldest so choose a sunny spot, avoiding any place where frost settles for frost-damaged flowers will not produce fruit. Strawberries are short-lived, and new plants should have a new bed.

SOIL

'The Strawberries in general love a
gentle hazelly loam, in which they will thrive
and bear greater plenty of fruit than in a
light rich soil. The ground should also be
moist, for if it is very dry, all the watering
which is given to the plants in warm dry seasons,
will not be sufficient to produce plenty of fruit.'

Philip Miller, FRS, 'The Gardeners Dictionary',
1768 edn

'A Profitable Strawberry' (Trafalgar), 1901

Strawberries like light, very fertile soil which holds moisture, but on damp patches they need good drainage, despite the fact that they are heavy drinkers. They will grow in a shallow soil, but again good watering during dry weather is mandatory. Soil should be slightly acid. A well manured patch where peas, beans or potatoes have been growing will suit strawberries. After forking over, leave the bed to settle down for a fortnight.

On heavy clays, initial deep cultivation is necessary with generous applications of humus. If you have really heavy clay soil, work the ground for several seasons before setting out the strawberries. The old Chilean strawberries do well in soil which is approaching clay. If you can get a few, they are fun to grow and will make you appreciate their modern descendants. Their fruits, incidentally, are odd-sized and rather ugly.

FERTILIZERS AND MANURING An average acre of strawberries absorbs nearly four times as much phosphate, three times as much potash and twice as much nitrate as an average acre of wheat, so soil rich in humus is necessary.

When the soil is rich in organic matter, such as well-rotted manure, compost or a high grade of coarse peat, no artificial fertilizers are needed. Following the first full harvest, apply a general fertilizer made by a reliable manufacturer at the rate recommended on the pack.

On sandy soils likely to be deficient in potash, spread 1oz per square yard (25g/sq m) of sulphate of potash. In subsequent years, apply half as much as this in February. Plants with slightly yellow-green leaves are claimed to crop best.

BUYING YOUR PLANTS

Pot-grown plants can be bought in August and September. Field-grown young plants are listed for sale in October/November or in the spring during March/April. The field-grown plants are usually cheaper than the potted ones, but the latter have good root growth and establish themselves more quickly.

To obtain top-quality crops, strawberries need to be replanted every three years, although many beds will produce for up to six years. Keen growers may want to restock after the second year.

When can you expect your new plants to have their first cropping year? Summer-fruiting varieties, such as 'Cambridge Vigour', if planted in the late summer or early autumn will produce fruit the following summer. If planted in the spring, then they should have the flowers removed in May so that they can build strength, cropping in the summer of the following year. Perpetuals should have their flowers removed during the first May after planting to ensure good fruiting in August.

The later the planting of either type in the autumn, the less will be the fruit in the maiden year (i.e., the following summer). If they are planted in the spring the first fruit will appear in the summer of the following year.

From the sowing of alpine seed to fruiting takes about eighteen months, although a few berries may be produced the first year.

PLANTING

Are your strawberries to grow in matted beds or in rows? Both methods find favour. In the matted-bed system, the runners from each plant are allowed to root. This results in a 'mat' of plants. To make picking easier, restrict the bed to 4ft (1.2m) wide, with the plants set in two rows 3ft (90cm) apart with 18in (45cm) between plants. While this system is a good one for the busy gardener, the beds do look untidy, routine cultivation is difficult, and the fruit produced can be smaller. If you have a large area needing ground cover, strawberries will quickly and attractively blanket it, and it is for this purpose that the matted-bed system is most useful.

From 'Herbarum Vivae Eicones',
1530

The perpetual strawberry, 'St Joseph'

The spaced-plant or row-planting system looks much neater and the plants can be easily controlled and tended when removing blossoms or runners. Set the plants 18in (45cm) from each other in rows at least 2ft (60cm) apart. Compact varieties, such as 'Elista' and 'Pantagruella' may be set more closely to each other, perhaps 9in (23cm) apart.

As soon as your plants arrive, unpack them and give them a good soak in water. If you are planting runners, soak the roots before planting. Then, in both cases, set out the plants at once. The crown of each plant should be just at ground level: on no account bury it too deep or cover any plant leaves.

WATERING

'In the first place the strawberry's chief need
is a great deal of water. In the second place,
it needs more water. In the third place,
I think I would give it a great deal more water.'

Marshall P. Wilder, in the Laxton Brothers' 'Strawberry Manual', 1899

Immediately after planting, water the bed. If the plants seem to wilt the next day, then water daily for the first week. Further watering should not be necessary except during very hot, dry periods.

After the fall of the petals, when the berries are forming, soak the soil thoroughly every seven to ten days, and again after the first harvest to encourage new growth. Avoid watering the plants during the height of the picking season as the wet berries may rot.

REMOVING FLOWERS

Remove any flowers of summer-fruiting varieties formed in the first May, if the plants were set out the previous late summer or autumn. With perpetuals, regardless of when planted, it is advisable to remove any flowers in the first May. After this first May, let the perpetuals flower at will.

REMOVING LEAVES

With summer-fruiting varieties, cut off and burn the old leaves after fruiting. If you have used straw around the plants, the bed may be burned. The next year's crop develops in the crown of the plant during mid-summer, so the removal of the old leaves should be done immediately picking has finished.

Remove the leaves on perpetuals each year after the final autumn picking.

PROPAGATION AND RUNNERS

Cut away all runners to increase strength in the parent plant and to prevent overcrowding.

In open rows remove the runners regularly. In matted beds, push the runners back into the row until a solid mat is established and, thereafter, remove any runners that stray outside the defined area of the bed. By removing the parent plant from time to time the matted bed will become self-renewing, assuming no viral diseases appear.

If your parent stock is free from virus symptoms, propagate your own new stock. Make a small nursery bed in which you will place some parent plants about 1yd (90cm) apart. These will not be for fruit production. Allow two or three runners from each parent and pin them to root in pots buried in the soil; pots should contain equal parts of loam, peat and sand.

In early August, when well rooted, the runners can easily be cut from the parent.

Runners left to grow directly in the soil can be planted out in their new beds in August, when good roots have developed.

WEEDING AND NETTING

Weed control in most strawberry beds is easily done by regular hoeing. If you think them necessary, chemical weedkillers can be helpful. Of the residual herbicides, strawberries are tolerant of Lenacil but less so of Simozine. If couch grass or ground elder appears, fork them out at once and do your best to keep these two persistent invaders at bay – it is unlikely you will ever vanquish them.

A temporary netting, as soon as the fruit show any colour, will protect the crop from birds. Plastic ¾in (2cm) mesh should be pulled over the bed and attached to low support posts at a height of not more than 1ft (30cm). Most garden beds are small enough that you can pick from either side simply by lifting the net and reaching in. An alternative solution to the bird problem is the use of a fruit cage.

TO OBTAIN CLEAN FRUIT

Just before the berries start to ripen, spread barley straw or a sheet of black polythene around the plants to prevent soil getting on the fruit. Do *not* put down either form of ground cover until the danger of frost is past, since covered soil absorbs far less of the sun's heat during the day.

PESTS AND DISEASES

APHIDS Usually found on leaves. Spray just before the flowers open, using a systemic such as Dimethoate or a contact spray such as Pyrethrum.
BIRDS Use netting, as described just above.
BOTRYTIS See under grey mould, below.
EELWORM These are so small that usually you cannot see them. They cause distortion of the plant and make the leaves crinkle. They are usually introduced to the soil by the planting of infected runners – another good reason for buying healthy certified stock – and can remain in the soil for some time. Treating the soil with a sterilant such as Basamid (Dazomet) may help, but it is usually best to concede defeat and open a new bed with

new plants, leaving the old ground to lie fallow but weedless for four to six months.

GREY MOULD (BOTRYTIS CINEREA) The wetter the weather at picking time, the worse is this disease. It appears on the fruit itself and poor air circulation encourages its development. Some varieties, such as 'Royal Sovereign', are more susceptible than others. For control, use Captan or Benlate when the flowers first open and then every seven to ten days until just before the fruit ripens.

LEAF HOPPERS These cause mottling of the leaves and can carry green-petal virus. Their presence can be recognized by the froth they produce, commonly called 'cuckoo spit'. Control either with aphicide spray or by removing leaves after the fruit has been harvested.

LEAF SPOT With this, red spots appear on mature leaves which gradually turn pale. Do not worry about the condition. If you cannot resist fussing, then spray with a Bordeaux mixture early in the spring.

MICE Mice enjoy eating strawberries. Buy a cat.

MILDEW This can affect the leaves, flowers and fruits, particularly in hot, dry weather. It appears first on the leaves, which curl and wither. Then a white-grey mould (which should not be confused with grey mould) develops on the fruit. Control by treating with Dinocap or Benlate. A good preventative step is to do so just before the plants flower and then afterwards.

RED-CORE DISEASE This is a fungus which debilitates and stunts plants. Leaves die and the roots are affected. It is a soil-borne disease which will not usually occur if you have bought certified stock. Control is drastic: dig up and burn the plants and abandon the bed.

RED SPIDER MITES Except in hot, dry conditions, these are not usually a threat. The symptom is a yellow mottling on the leaves. Control by spraying with Malathion *before* flowering; and, if the plants are cloched, keep them watered.

SLUGS A hole in a berry is probably the sign of a marauding slug. Control using slug pellets or Draza, bearing in mind that both are poisonous to man and beast.

STRAWBERRY MITES These creatures are beyond the human eye, feeding on the surface of the leaves and making them twist and curl. The effects are usually noticeable in July and August. Prevent this condition by spraying with nicotine solution in May.

VIRAL DISEASES A number of viruses can affect strawberries, causing stunting and a poor crop – if any crop at all. Symptoms are yellowing edges, blotching and crumbling of the leaves. To control, dig up and burn the plants and start a new bed elsewhere. Next time make sure to buy certified new stock.

WASPS These will not be troublesome with summer-ripened fruits, but the later perpetuals attract them. Forget commercial sprays and try to share your crop as painlessly as possible with these insects.

If you have to clear a strawberry bed, the advice of the 1837 *British Flora Medica* still applies: foliage is eaten by sheep and goats but not liked by cows and 'refused by horses and swine'. For what it is worth, my own goats ignore the leaves but gratefully plunder all the berries.

STRAWBERRIES FOR DECORATION

Vegetables and fruits can be as decorative in the garden as flowers. A strawberry barrel can be sited on a patio or terrace, as a centre-piece in a small town garden or just outside the kitchen door. Its continuous flowers and berries will be as bright as a small bed of summer flowers – and give you pounds of delicious fruit into the bargain. The berries will remain clean and dry and beyond the reach of slugs.

Garden centres sell purpose-made barrels, but it is easy enough to drill some holes in a sound wooden one. Make enough holes for about thirty plants. These holes need to be about 2½in (6.5cm) in diameter and 1ft (30cm) apart. Stagger them so that the plants are not in rows around the barrel. You will also need holes in the base about 1in (2.5cm) across and 6in (15cm) apart for drainage.

To ensure that water flows evenly to all the plants, put a pipe filled with stones down the centre of the barrel. Once all the plants are in, pull out the pipe, leaving the stones. Stand the barrel on bricks so that excess water can drain away.

To prepare for the soil, cover the inside bottom of the barrel with a 2in (5cm) layer of broken brick, stone or rock. To fill the barrel use a rich soil with plenty of old manure and some bonemeal. If you cannot get manure, use a commercial fertilizer.

Fill the barrel up to the first series of holes. Firmly set in the plants,

threading the roots in from the outside and leaving the crown at the level of the hole. Spread the roots, then fill in with soil up to the next level, pressing firmly. Repeat the planting process until you get to the top level, making sure at each stage that the soil is firmly pressed down. Place plants in the soil at the very top to make a 'lid'.

You can use summer-fruiting strawberries or perpetuals – 'Gento' is a good choice. You can, of course, mix varieties to give a long harvest and display season.

The only work after planting is to pinch out runners and weed the top. Your strawberry barrel will last for three years. Remember that your summer slogan must be 'Constant Watering'.

Besides the strawberry barrel, other good containers include vertical-display 'towerpots', which hold up to twelve plants, are easily watered and make a pretty show. Ordinary earthenware and plastic pots will do the job too – in fact, any container works so long as it is kept well watered.

STRAWBERRIES FOR LIMITED SPACE

. . . returning, visited one Mr. Tombs's Garden, it
has large noble Walks, some modern statues; but what
was prettiest was the Vine-yard planted in
Strawberry-borders, staked at 10 foote distance.
John Evelyn's diary, 8th May, 1654

Take a tip from Evelyn's comment and make a row of plants alongside your garden path, by the edge of a terrace or around the sunny edge of a flower bed.

Duchesne recommended 'planting between rows of beans to get better value from the land'. In biodynamic practice strawberries are often accompanied by a favourite companion plant, pine trees. Hence, it is said that a pine-needle mulch makes the berries taste more like wild ones.

Limited space often produces imaginative gardens, and strawberries lend themselves to artful designing. In 1650, for example, Claude Mollet suggested using all sorts of low-growing flowers, including white and red strawberries, in little compartments to give the overall impression of a Turkish carpet.

And what of 'climbing' strawberries? It was on 22nd July, 1956, that Vita Sackville-West first mentioned in her weekly newspaper column that rumours were reaching Britain from the Continent of a strange new 'climbing' variety. She wrote that 'if you bought a plant in Switzerland or Germany or France you had to give your word of honour that you would not bring it away'.

Today the so-called 'climbing' strawberry, 'Hummel', is widely sold. You can train it up a post or against a trellis, and it can reach 6ft (1.8m) in height. Another variety suitable for trellis training or support by the tying up of its runners is the aptly named 'Mount Everest'.

KEEPING QUALITIES

Dry berries travel best and those picked in the cool of the morning keep better. With an ever-increasing number of cultivars, the advancement of scientific methods and greater knowledge of the origins of diseases, strawberry researchers continue to pile up an impressive volume of studies including how best to improve keeping qualities. But none of this changes the fact that the shorter the distance and the time between the strawberry being picked and you eating it, the better.

JUDGING YOUR HARVEST

The best yardstick by which to judge your harvest is your enjoyment of it. However:

The sizes of strawberries vary. The fruits of some are uniformly large and of others uniformly small. Some bear large fruits at the first picking, after which the berries are small (this is regarded as an undesirable characteristic).

The commonest shapes are conical, oblong, oblate, round and wedge-shaped.

The seeds in a good fruit should be few and small, and yellow seeds are more attractive than darker ones.

Strawberries from 'Pomona Britannica', 1804–12.
Left, 'Hovey'; right, 'Chile'; below left, 'Scarlet Alpine';
below right, 'Scarlet Flesh Pine'

The colours of strawberries vary from white to red and from red to dark maroon, the white varieties being usually blushed with pink. Dark-coloured berries show bruises less than light-coloured ones. A white tip on a dark berry is considered a defect.

Flavours can be sweet, neutral or flat, sub-acid, tart or sour. Climate greatly modifies flavour and soil has a noticeable though lesser effect.

All strawberries are more or less aromatic and their fragrance is a good guide to their worth. Smell is, after all, the most faithful of all our senses – 'The only one', Colette wrote, 'that will not compromise.'

THE PERFECT STRAWBERRY

Quality in a strawberry is a balanced combination of colour, flavour, smell and texture. Just as we pick our friends, so we must choose the variety that most pleases us. There is only one perfect strawberry in existence and that is the strawberry of memory. We can find no fault in this favourite fruit of childhood.

And yet, when each summer comes, we can know again why the strawberry was once called the 'fruit of the blessed'.

A STRAWBERRY CALENDAR

This calendar is from Mary Spiller's excellent *Growing Fruit*, published by Allen Lane in 1980.

FEBRUARY
Cover some plants with cloches or polythene tunnels for early fruiting; Apply complete fertilizer

MARCH
Hoe as soon as soil dry enough and whenever weeds appear

APRIL
Ventilate covered strawberries when in flower and on hot days; Spray against aphids and mildew before flowering and when necessary; De-runner fruiting beds

MAY
Spot-treat perennial weeds; Spray against botrytis and repeat at 7–10 day intervals; Water

JUNE
De-runner fruiting beds; Water; Straw; Net; Pick fruit

JULY
Remove net when picking finished; Cut or burn off leaves after crop finished; Water; Pin down runners on plants grown for propagation

AUGUST
Hoe

SEPTEMBER
Cover late-fruiting varieties with cloches to prolong fruiting

OCTOBER
Hoe if soil dry enough

NOVEMBER–FEBRUARY
Fork if weedy and too wet to hoe, and give dressing of bulky organic material

EARLY AND LATE FRUITS
If plants are covered with glass, cloches or polythene tunnels in early February, ripe strawberries become possible up to three weeks earlier than usual. To ensure satisfactory pollination, ventilate the plants during their flowering season. Use the cloches again in late September: place them over perpetual varieties to save them from frost damage. This will add two or three weeks to the cropping season.

ACKNOWLEDGEMENTS

I am grateful to many for their help in my hunt for the strawberry, not least those at the British Library and the London Library. My special thanks, however, to Dr Brent Elliot, Librarian of the Lindley Library, the Royal Horticultural Society; Rosemary Elwes, Curator of the Embroiderers' Guild Collection, Hampton Court Palace; Kate Jones, Librarian of the Royal Society of Health; Arthur MacGregor, Assistant Keeper in Antiquities, the Ashmolean Museum, Oxford; and especially Graham Nicholson whose wide knowledge of food and cooking was of considerable assistance.

I would also like to thank the following for their permission to reproduce: 'The Strawberry Plant' from *Selected Poems* by Jon Silkin, by kind permission of Routledge & Kegan Paul PLC; 'Middle East Strawberry Jam' from *A Book of Middle Eastern Food*, by kind permission of Claudia Roden; 'Fraises Sarah Bernhardt' from *Ma Cuisine* by Auguste Escoffier © Ernest Flammarion 1934 © English text, The Hamlyn Publishing Group Ltd, 1965; 'Les Crèmes aux Fraises de Bois' from *French Provincial Cooking* by Elizabeth David, by kind permission of David Higham Associates Ltd, and 'Compôte of Strawberries with Almond Milk', by kind permission of Elizabeth David and Prospect Books Ltd; 'Pure Essence of Arabian Nights' from *Aromas & Flavours of Past and Present* by Alice B. Toklas, by kind permission of Michael Joseph; 'Strawberries with Lemon' from *Cooking with Pomaine*, edited and translated by Peggie Benton, by kind permission of Faber & Faber Ltd; 'Red Red Strawberry Jam' from *The Joy of Cooking* by Irma S. Rombauer, by kind permission of J. M. Dent & Sons Ltd; 'Salad Elona', by kind permission of Jane Grigson and Penguin Books Ltd.

The publishers would like to thank the following for the loan of items for photographs by David Cripps on pages 42, 51, 60, 62, 66, 73, 100, 102: Ruth Baum, Thimble Specialists, 63 Cranbourne Gardens, NW11, 102; Nina Campbell, Walton Street, SW3, 66; Crabtree & Evelyn Ltd, 60; Richard Dennis, Kensington Church Street, W8, 42, 73; Halcyon Days Ltd, Bruton Street, W1, 102; The Lacquer Chest, Kensington Church Street, W8, 100; Robert Opie Collection, 51, 60, 62; Stafford Whiteaker, 100.

Acknowledgements for Illustrations: American Museum in Britain, Bath, 29, 102B; Ariel Press Ltd, 9L; Ashmolean Museum, Oxford, 96; Betty Luton White collection, 104; Bodleian Library, Oxford, 77, 79, 95BL, BR; Bridgeman Art Library/Guildhall, London, 6; Bridgeman Art Library/Prado Museum, Madrid, 23, 91; British Library, Title, 11, 18, 31, 32, 37L and R, 104R, 109, 111L, 115, 116, 123; British Museum, 9R; Christie's, 39, 99B; Elizabeth David, Half-title page; 'Dictionnaire Encyclopédique de l'Epicerie' by Albert Seigneurie, Paris 1904, 49; Embroiderers' Guild, 92BL; Fotomas Index, 13, 80, 111R; Knopf Publishers, New York, 35; Mansell Collection, 43, 61, 114; Museum of English Rural Life, University of Reading, 15; Mrs Lesley O'Malley, 102; Paperchase, 58; Royal Horticultural Society/Lindley Library, Frontisp., 19, 27, 36; Sotheby's, 94; 'Strawberry and Bee' by Graham Rust (1983), Spink & Son Ltd, by kind permission of the Hon. Mrs Morrison, 124B; Victoria & Albert Museum, Crown Copyright, 92T, BR; by permission of the Trustees of the Wallace Collection, 87; © 1918 Frederick Warne, London (by permission of the publishers), 54; Josiah Wedgwood & Sons Ltd, 99T; Stafford Whiteaker, 43, 101, 104, 107; Whitney Museum of American Art, New York/gift of Edgar Williams & Bernice Chrysler Garbisch, 65.

INDEX

Page numbers in *italics* refer to illustrations

INDEX